# *He Can* HEAL

# *He Can* HEAL

*From the depths of sorrow
to the joy of love and forgiveness*

**GARY CERAN**

Covenant Communications, Inc.

Cover image: *Foggy sunrise - Lonely tree and Sun* © konradlew, courtesy www.istockphoto.com.

Cover design copyright © 2014 by Covenant Communications, Inc.

Published by Covenant Communications, Inc.
American Fork, Utah

Copyright © 2014 by Gary Ceran
All rights reserved. No part of this book may be reproduced in any format or in any medium without the written permission of the publisher, Covenant Communications, Inc., P.O. Box 416, American Fork, UT 84003. This work is not an official publication of The Church of Jesus Christ of Latter-day Saints. The views expressed within this work are the sole responsibility of the author and do not necessarily reflect the position of The Church of Jesus Christ of Latter-day Saints, Covenant Communications, Inc., or any other entity.

Printed in the United States of America
First Printing: May 2014

20 19 18 17 16 15 14 10 9 8 7 6 5 4 3 2 1

ISBN 978-1-62108-473-0

To the family I lost,
To the family I found,
And to love that lasts forever!

# Acknowledgments

I ALWAYS IMAGINED THAT WRITING one's memoirs was a very *personal* thing. Although I knew that reopening old wounds would be hard, I still figured the process itself would be easy. It was certainly something I thought I could do on my own, so I began. As time went on, however, I discovered—much to my dismay—that trying to condense decades of sorrows, joys, life lessons, and miracles into a concise, interesting, and meaningful book that people would actually want to read wasn't quite so easy. When, after many months, the writing itself seemed to be finished at last, it became evident that the process was a lot more complicated than I'd thought. I quickly learned that designing, typesetting, publishing, printing, and marketing a finished volume required the insights, talents, and labor of many beyond myself. To all those who have contributed those special gifts to help this work come to fruition, to improve it, or to expand its reach, I offer my most sincere gratitude. Among those, I express special thanks to my editor, Stacey Owen, who has done so much to make this book better. I also want to express my gratitude to my sister-in-law, Annie Jensen, and others who read my initial manuscript. Thank you for seeing its potential and believing this to be a story worth telling. My hope and prayer is that this book will honor their vision by blessing the lives of many readers who have been, are, or will yet be called upon to pass through difficult trials. I especially hope it helps *you*.

With all my heart, I thank my beloved wife, Corrine, for her encouragement, her confidence in me, her willingness to sacrifice, and her ability to trust that our loving Heavenly Father would sustain us as I took time off work to write. She has done to the pages of this book what the Father, through trials, has done to His children—made them better. With a perfect balance of tough love and tender care, she and Father have each polished, refined, and improved what they already loved so much from the start.

Corky is in many ways the very reason this book exists. Without her goading I may have never completed it, and without the joy of her companionship, I may have never found its happy ending. My wife is the greatest blessing I have ever received in this life. She and the many miracles that have come into my life both because of her and along with her stand as blessed reminders to me of Heavenly Father's love. Her companionship is a gift of mercy, and her love is a cherished treasure. Her example inspires me, her prayers sustain me, her testimony lifts me, and her red pen reminds me that I tend to use too many words to say too little. For all of this and so much more, I love her . . . now and forever!

I also thank you, the reader, for believing that it is possible to learn vicariously from the struggles and ultimate victories of another, albeit a very ordinary brother in the gospel of Jesus Christ. I pray that the Lord will reward your faith with understanding and peace.

May you be blessed as you read with a greater ability to see your own unique troubles with a more eternal perspective, and may that vision give you the strength and courage to endure whatever personalized problems the Lord may provide to test and grow your faith.

God lives. He knows you. He loves you. And He desires what is best for you *in every instance*. Trust Him! If you give Him your heart, He will work mighty miracles in your life! Be sure to thank Him when those miracles come.

Above all, therefore, I thank my loving Father in Heaven, who *is* "above all." I thank Him for this world of joys and sorrows, for the freedom to choose, and for the opportunity to change. I thank Him for the trials that shape our lives and the pains that introduce us to a greater depth of feeling. I thank Him for His Son, Jesus Christ, who, by His Atonement, bears all our sins and sorrows and who, by His Resurrection and plan of happiness, allows us to live eternally as families. I thank Him for sending love to heal our hearts and for keeping His promise of joy in the morning. And I thank Him for this wonderful life, for through its years of tutoring, heart-softening, soul-stretching, life-shaping experiences, He both allows and helps us to be blessed by our trials.

# Foreword

ONE BY ONE, WELL-WISHERS WALKED reverently past three open caskets. Some came to say good-bye to the little girl in the first one—a carefree, bright-eyed angel with long, flowing curls, who had sung and danced and smiled her way into the heart of every person who knew her. For seven and a half years, Julianna had been my "little princess."

Even more came to honor the boy in the second casket—a gifted, rugged, spiritual man-child whose light and laughter filled whatever room he was in. For nearly sixteen years, Ian had been one of my very best friends, my "little buddy."

Still more came to pay tribute to the woman in the last casket. She was the sweetest and kindest of women. There were many who referred to her as the most Christlike person they had ever known. For twenty-one years my wife, Cheryl, had been my *everything*!

Every one of the sweet people in that line had come to comfort the three of us who survived the accident, but as is so often the case in such circumstances, it seemed to fall more upon *us* to comfort *them*. We hugged each person as they passed through the line, mourned with them, wiped away their tears, and bore solemn testimonies to them of our Savior's love and of peace that surpasses all understanding. As we did so, it occurred to me that all of those who were at that viewing as well as tens of thousands of others who had heard through the media of the Christmas Eve tragedy that had taken the lives of our loved ones, understood our pain, for many truly felt it with us. What they could *not* seem to understand or feel with us was the comfort, the witness, the understanding, and the peace that came with and sprang from that pain.

I looked down the line that, even after several hours, still went from one end of our church to the other and out the door. Seeing the pain etched in so many kind faces, I wished I could find a way to help them understand.

As I turned back to greet the next person, my eyes met those of a woman I had never seen before. Sullenly, almost solemnly, she came closer. Through her tears, she offered her condolences and told of how she had read about our recent tragedy—and previous ones—in the newspaper.

"I don't know how you do it!" she said, weeping as she shared how she had struggled for years with the trial of her own faith. Then she looked right into my eyes and said, "You should write a book."

I had often brushed aside comments like that as some sort of sincere, kind, yet somewhat morbid flattery. It always felt as if people were complimenting me for having such a hard life. But for some reason, this woman's words pierced my heart and reverberated in my mind. I knew she wasn't trying to flatter me; she was *pleading* with me. In that instant it occurred to me that I had never really put those two thoughts together before:

"I don't know how you do it."

"You should write a book."

Like so many others, this good woman had suffered every bit as much as I had, if not more. What she lacked, I realized, was not experience, but an understanding of how to *cope with* and *grow from* that experience. Everyone has trials, but not everyone has answers. As a result, many people suffer unnecessarily for years because they simply do not know how to allow their life to be blessed by adversity. That is why I decided to write this book.

Often, after I have spoken to a large group, dozens of people come up and share their personal trials and tragedies with me. It breaks my heart to hear some of the terrible things good people are called upon to endure day after day. So many of them struggle to cope and eventually buckle under the terrible weight of overwhelming burdens. Many suffer in silence. Most feel alone. Some feel like giving up. If you are one of those who is crying out for help, feeling that no one understands, do not despair! There is One who knows your pain because He has borne it.

Annie Swetchine said, "Those who have suffered much are like those who know many languages; they have learned to understand and be understood by all."[1] Jesus is the ultimate example of that. I hope that the little I share here is also understood and that it will truly bless your life.

Why, you may ask, would I take on so monumental a task as to write about the most difficult, heart-wrenching, soul-stretching experiences of my life? What would prompt me to pour the lemon juice of recollection and the salt of public scrutiny into my life's wounds? I want to help you.

I pray that these few words of insight and encouragement will buoy up your faith and give you a little more strength to endure. Emily Dickinson said beautifully:

*If I can stop one heart from breaking,*
*I shall not live in vain;*
*If I can ease one life the aching,*
*Or cool one pain,*
*Or help one fainting robin*
*Unto his nest again,*
*I shall not live in vain.*[2]

My specific trials may not be yours; nevertheless, I know that the principles which have comforted me and provided me with answers as I have sought to understand suffering's high and glorious purposes apply equally to all of the trials common to man. As you seek to understand the purposes of your own particular trials and as you strive to discover and develop the character traits that your afflictions were *tailored* to create in you, remember there is One who knows you perfectly. He understands all of your trials, and He knows all of your yearnings and all of your pain, for He descended below them all. He is "a man of sorrows, acquainted with grief,"[3] and He loves you with an infinite love. That person is our Savior and Redeemer, the Lord Jesus Christ. Because He has descended below all things, He knows how to succor each of us and give us the peace and blessed relief we so desperately need.

Turn to Him. Trust Him. Rely on Him, and you will find that all you suffer will turn to your good. Then you can look back on all of the hardest experiences of your life and realize you were not only blessed *with* adversity but *by* it.

# Prologue

On Christmas Eve 2006, I gathered my wife and four children from our cast party and ushered them into our family car. Earlier that evening Clarissa, Caleb, and I had finished our last performance of Charles Dickens's play *A Christmas Carol* at Utah's Hale Centre Theatre in West Valley City. My wife, Cheryl, had looked on from the audience with our other two children, Ian and Julianna.

As we said our final good-byes and piled into our little Mercury Sable, we breathed a sigh of relief. We had worked so hard to make Christmas special for the thousands who came to see the play. Now it was finally *our* time, and we were eager to go home and spend the holidays together. Our sacrifices had filled us with a deep sense of satisfaction, but the time we'd spent apart had been difficult. It was wonderful for us to all be together again as we always had been before.

We decided to stop for a few last-minute presents and some of the special ingredients that made our traditional Christmas Eve dinner so wonderful. We took far longer than expected, but at long last we headed toward the freeway to make our way home. The children were all sleeping peacefully in the car, no doubt dreaming of the good times we would share and the memories we would make together over the next two days. I looked at them fondly, my heart full of love and contentment. I thought to myself, *This will be a Christmas like no other.*

It certainly *would* be, for a few minutes later, in a moment when we least expected it, fate handed us a trial that would change our lives forever. This is the true story of that tragic Christmas *past* and an unexpected Christmas *present* that came as a result.

The following day the sun arose as it always had before, but nothing else would ever be the same.

The nature and timing of our very public tragedy stunned the community. News of the awful losses our family had previously endured added to the shock. Moved by compassion and inspired by one simple act of forgiveness, many turned their focus to the true "reason for the season." This was a Christmas when *Christ* mattered more than ever. Inspired by that Giver of all good gifts, many would open their hearts and set in motion countless acts of compassion, forgiveness, and Christlike service.

I have written this book in hopes of sharing some of the answers I have found to life's most difficult questions: How does one cope with the tutoring and soul-stretching trials of life? How is it possible to forgive someone who has robbed you and those you love of what is most precious and has caused you such unspeakable pain? Why would a loving Father in Heaven allow such suffering?

I hope that you will see parallels to your own life and grow in your faith as I have grown in mine.

# 1
## Just Like the Cratchits

The audience of more than five hundred patrons was abuzz with eager anticipation as they settled noisily into their seats. Parents scrambled to gather children who had run out to the lobby for some last-minute treats. Senior patrons whose discipline and more settled lives allowed them to arrive early sat with warm smiles and calmly perused their playbills, learning what they could about each member of the cast. Couples, both young and old, having just come in from the frosty winter weather outside, snuggled together, enjoying each other's warmth and the charm of the theater's ambiance. On every side people chattered with excitement about presents they had just purchased, gift wrapping they had yet to do, and all of the sundry stresses and wonders the next day would hold. Newer patrons motioned around the theater in awe, pointing out piece after piece of the stunning scenery and props that had converted our theater-in-the-round into the streets of Victorian England. Bob Cratchit was getting ready to race in late to the office of Scrooge and Marley. I knew this, you see, because I was Bob Cratchit.

As the ushers helped the last few stragglers to their seats and began to close the entrance curtains at the top of the theater, a hush quickly swept over the crowd. Those in the audience who had seen this production many times before knew what kind of amazing spectacle awaited them. When first-timers heard in a brief preshow announcement that *A Christmas Carol* at Hale had been honored as the fourth best thing to do at Christmastime *in the entire country,* their excitement built to a crescendo. One thing was certain: *everyone* could feel the magic of Christmas that hung in the air. For the next two hours, everything else—shopping lists, traffic jams, malls, and all of life's everyday stresses—would simply melt away. These fortunate few were about to leave behind a world of cares and witness the magical redemption of Ebenezer Scrooge.

After my daughter Clarissa, my son Caleb, and I finished quietly warming up in the wings for the song in the opening scene, I tiptoed silently toward the stage. Parting the curtains of "vom 2" (one of the stage's three entrance corridors) just enough to make a hole the size of a quarter, I peeked out, making sure to remain unnoticed by the audience. Looking just beyond the stage, I scanned the crowd until I found my family. There, in three seats near the top of the theater, Cheryl, my sweet wife of twenty-one wonderful years; our son Ian, barely a month shy of his sixteenth birthday; and our little seven-and-a-half-year-old daughter, Julianna, sat eagerly awaiting the dimming of the lights that would signal the start of the play.

Cheryl smiled warmly as she sat with her arm around little Julie. Ian, who loved Christmas as much as any man who ever lived, sat straight and tall, soaking it all in. Of course, they had seen us do *A Christmas Carol* many times before, but tonight they looked forward to it even more than usual. It was December 23—our last performance of the run. When this show was over, it would mark an end to three long months of evenings away. At last the family would all be together again and our *real* Christmas season could finally begin!

It always felt natural for me to play Bob Cratchit. For years, I worked in accounting and finance, and at times I even felt as if I had the same kind of working relationship with some of my bosses that Cratchit endured with Scrooge. Like the Cratchits, we were never rich. At times our feasts were modest, but like the Cratchits, we were always grateful for whatever gifts the Lord provided. Like the Cratchits, our home was full of love—a place of warmth, joy, and peace. Like the Cratchits, we ached and yearned, we read the scriptures together, we laughed, and we sang. Like the Cratchits, we knew both the torture and the reward of caring for a sickly child. But there was one thing even more powerful than all the rest: like the Cratchits, we knew what it meant to bury a child.

There is one especially emotional scene in Dickens's *A Christmas Carol* that I seemed uniquely well-suited to portray on stage. Our director, John Sweeney, always called it the "Sad Cratchit" scene. This was the part when Scrooge was shown a crutch without an owner and a not-too-distant day when Bob would yearn in vain to hold his beloved son in his arms. Our director's instructions were very clear: "You mustn't play this scene as if you are outwardly sad. Though on the inside you are brokenhearted, on the outside you have to force a smile. For the sake of your family, you must try to hide the hurt."

I knew exactly what he was talking about because I had done it many times myself.

After losing precious Tiny Tim, Mrs. Cratchit and her surviving children are sitting together by the fire. Their husband and father, Bob, should have already been home long ago, but as his young son Peter points out, "I think he has walked a little slower than he used to these past few evenings, Mother."[4]

Perhaps some of you know how the sadness and emptiness that follow the loss of a loved one—particularly a child—tend to make an already heavy burden seem even more difficult to bear. Depression drains your energy, your step slows, your shoulders slouch, your head droops, your eyes darken, and it feels like there's a fifty-pound sack strapped around your heart. I knew how to act that feeling because I had *lived* it. So each night, as the Cratchit family sat huddled together, waiting for the head of their home to arrive, I would stand off in the wings, revisiting the handful of heart-wrenching moments in my life that made Bob Cratchit's pain so very real to me. Other actors would sometimes stop and watch me, at times concerned but always respectful. As I stood offstage behind the curtain, with my head lowered, fighting back tears as I remembered the hardest trials of my life, onstage Mrs. Cratchit, ever trying to be positive, would acknowledge Peter's comment, recalling with gentle fondness how, when Tiny Tim was on Bob's shoulders, she had often seen him walk "very fast . . . very fast indeed."[5] Her heart aches and her love swells. In that beautifully nostalgic moment, she notices Bob as he comes through the door. One by one she and the children rush to greet him with warm hugs, pretending as best they can to be happy and upbeat. Mrs. Cratchit holds her frigid husband tenderly for a moment then ushers him toward the hearth.

"Come, and warm yourself by the fire."

His eldest daughter, Martha (played by *my* eldest daughter, Clarissa), offers him a warm drink. "That will warm you."[6]

Still shivering from the chill outside, he takes the copper cup from his daughter, blows away some steam, then takes a few soothing sips. Warmed both inside and out by his daughter's gesture to comfort him, he smiles at Martha. "Thank you, my dear."[7]

For a moment he warms his hands with the cup then turns to place it on the mantel. As he does, he just happens to notice the crutch once held by his beloved Tiny Tim. Unable to bear the sight of it, he quickly turns back to the family. He notices that everyone, like him, is terribly sad.

Filled with compassion, he decides to try to cheer them all up by quickly talking of something happy. With feigned excitement, he points to the scraggly little Christmas tree that sits on the mantel, and he exclaims, "Well . . . I see you've all been very busy today! Yes, the tree is nearly as pleasant as the yew that . . ."[8] He stops himself midsentence, realizing what he is about to say. His exuberant, pretended happiness immediately turns to unguarded sadness. "As pleasant as the yew that stands over Tim."[9]

His countenance falls, and his voice tapers as he realizes he has just revealed that he's been to visit Tim's grave. Mrs. Cratchit rushes to his side to buoy him up.

"You went today, then, Robert?"[10] she asks, desperately trying to sound happy and excited.

"Yes, my dear. I wish you could have gone. It would have done you good to see how green a place it is. But you'll see it often. I promised him that I would walk there on a Sunday."[11]

His voice tapers off in embarrassment that he has been talking to a son who is no longer there. He stares off and, all at once, breaks down. Dickens wrote, "Bob couldn't help it. If he could have helped it, he and his child would have been farther apart perhaps than they were."[12] Weeping, Cratchit utters a woeful lament, "My child . . . my dear little child!"

Moved by his pain, Mrs. Cratchit, so faithful and compassionate, takes his arm to comfort him. Although she tries to hide it, it is obvious that she suffers just as he does. Mercifully, their young son Frederick, touched by his father's suffering, rushes over to comfort him. "Don't mind it, Father! Don't be grieved!"[13]

Bob is startled from his tears and inspired by his son's show of strength. Warmed by his son's courage, touched by the boy's innocent plea, and wanting so badly to put on a good face for his family, he wipes his eyes, manages to force a little grin, and replies to his boy, "I'm alright now. Thank you, my dears."[14]

This was all so familiar to me!

Coming home from work every day after losing a child was something I knew all too well. I had done it for years. Usually I was greeted in much the same way as Bob Cratchit had been—first, soothed by the love and kind words of a tender wife, who cared more for my happiness and comfort than her own; next, mobbed by children, who hugged me with so much love and exuberance that it all seemed to hurt a little less. Then, we all did our best to put on happy faces and talk of something upbeat.

It seemed like no matter which way I turned in my house, my eyes would somehow seem to land on something that affected me like Tiny Tim's crutch affected Bob. Often when I least expected it, the tiniest thing could suddenly send me—or any of us for that matter—into an emotional tailspin full of painfully wonderful and wonderfully painful memories of someone who was gone. But if any of us ever grew *too* sad, the others would all swarm to them and engulf them in love and attention. Positive, uplifting conversations would typically ensue, just like the one Bob had with his family about a kindly visitor who had tried to fill his day with cheer: "Mr. Scrooge's nephew, Master Fred, was in today as he always is at Christmas. I think he is the pleasantest spoken gentleman I have ever known!"[15]

How important good people are in our lives! What a gift it is that the Lord sends them to lift us up and inspire us! Over the years I have known many people like Fred, including the man who played his role, Dave Petersen, a soft-spoken and wonderful man who I worked with in the Church Office Building for nearly twenty years.

Bob elaborates on the happy encounter, telling the family more about his chance meeting with Fred: "I am heartily sorry for it, Mr. Cratchit, and heartily sorry for your good wife."[16]

Then, with a wry little grin, Bob adds, "By the bye, how he knew that I'll never know!"[17]

"Knew what, my dear?" asks Mrs. Cratchit.

"Why, that you are a good wife!"[18] jokes Bob.

Peter immediately jumps up in her defense: "Everybody knows that!"[19]

Caught in the absurdity of his well-intended jest, Bob laughs knowingly and confirms that his son is right: "Very well observed my boy! I should hope they do!"[20] Then Cratchit goes on with his story, "'Heartily sorry for your good wife. If I can be of service to you in any way,' he said—giving me his card, 'pray come to me.' It really seemed as if he had known our Tiny Tim and grieved with us."[21]

It was often the same for me. Over time I learned that receiving bits of happy small talk or words of sympathy and encouragement always seemed to help my wife and children, just as it did Bob's. And my sweet wife, Cheryl, would always respond with kind words for those who wished us well, just as Mrs. Cratchit did.

"I'm sure he's a good soul!"[22] suggests Mrs. Cratchit.

With his characteristic optimism, Bob replies, "You would be *surer* of it, my dear, if you saw and spoke to him. I shouldn't be at all surprised—mark what I say—if he got Peter a better situation!"[23]

Mrs. Cratchit, now filled with *genuine* excitement for her son, moves toward him and exclaims, "Only hear that, Peter!"[24]

Beside him Belinda nudges him as she teases, "And then Peter will be keeping company with someone, and setting up for himself!"[25]

Bob joins with the rest of the family in laughing at the idea of his young son soon having a family of his own. Peter was just a small boy (played by *my* small boy, Caleb).

"Get along with you!"[26] retorts Peter, grinning.

Thoughtfully, Bob kneels down to reassure him. As he looks into his son's eyes and sees a flash of the man the boy will someday become, Bob thinks of how quickly time passes and shakes his head. Then, placing his hand on Peter's knee, he reluctantly acknowledges, "It's just as likely as not . . . one of these days, though there's plenty of time for that."[27]

Now grinning, Bob stands and walks toward the fireplace, still amused at the thought of little Peter growing up but suddenly also a bit thoughtful. As he approaches the hearth and looks at the mantel, he notices once again the small wooden crutch that Tiny Tim had always used to limp along. Lovingly, he picks it up. As he does, his mind is besieged by a flood of memories of his absent son. Overcome with emotion, he turns back, struggling to fight back his tears. He looks at Peter then suddenly turns away and stares off blankly. His voice fades as he says, "Plenty of time . . ."[28]

In an extraordinary moment of powerful, raw emotion, Bob realizes that he had always said the same thing about Tiny Tim. There would be "plenty of time" for him to earn the money needed to heal his son; "plenty of time" for Tim to get well; "plenty of time" for them to enjoy life together; "plenty of time." But there wasn't.

Overcome with grief—and guilt—the heartbroken father realizes, as each of us eventually does, how quickly time passes. Tears begin to well up in Bob's eyes as he holds the crutch in front of him, looks heavenward, and remembers the child he had held so often.

Reverently and soberly he counsels his family, "But however and whenever we are parted from one another, we shall always remember this *first* parting, and shall not quarrel easily among ourselves, and forget poor Tiny Tim in doing it, shall we?"[29]

His youngest daughter, Harriet, stands up straight and tall and boldly declares, "Never, Father. Never!"[30]

He picks up his precious girl and holds her close. "Then I am happy . . . very happy indeed."

Suddenly blessed with a new perspective, a loving father who had been struggling with the death of one of his children reaches out to embrace one of those whom the Lord has left to comfort him, and love begins to heal his heart.

The lights fade to black, and in the darkness, the scene changes to the churchyard where Tiny Tim is buried. As the lights come up, Mr. and Mrs. Cratchit are standing before the grave of their little son. Struggling to bear the heartache, Bob begins to sing a familiar Christmas carol:

"So bring Him incense, gold and myrrh,
Come peasant, king to own Him."

As he begins the next line of the song, he breaks down and falls to his knees. His voice falters as he begins to weep uncontrollably. Mrs. Cratchit, ever by his side, tries to strengthen his faith by continuing the song for him, sweetly proclaiming the reassuring words:

"The King of Kings salvation brings!
Let loving hearts enthrone Him!"

The center of the stage beneath them rises, symbolically lifting them up, and they are suddenly encircled by a glorious choir of powerful, angelic voices praising God and singing:

"This, this is Christ the King,
Whom Shepherds guard and angels sing,
Haste, haste to bring him laud,
The Babe, the Son of Mary!"[31]

Bob clutches the crutch, his last physical reminder of Tim.

Openly weeping, the man gazes heavenward toward the loving home in which his son has at last found healing and rest. And finally, in an act that symbolizes the surrendering of his heart to God, he lets go of the one thing he had left to hang onto; he lays Tim's crutch on the grave and grieves.

And so it had been with us. Over the years my wife and children and I had known this same sorrow ourselves. We had known the pain and grief that come with loss, and we had been blessed with the unifying love that grew out of strengthening each other . . . just like the Cratchits.

# 2

## So Grateful to Be with My Family

At four o'clock that afternoon, we heard Tiny Tim say his famous final line for the last time: "God bless us—every one!"[32]

With a hearty amen and with the play's long run finally over, we scrambled to fill the next few hours catching up on neglected traditions, doing last minute shopping, having a few unexpected but joyful reunions, and keeping a few long-postponed promises. After a busy afternoon, we went back to the theater for our cast party. We spent a few hours reminiscing about missed lines and bloopers, costume malfunctions, and—most of all—conversations with patrons whose hearts had been touched. When we were done eating, we wished everyone a Merry Christmas and said our good-byes before heading for the door.

We were all smiles as the six of us hugged the members of the cast on our way to the corridor. Ian, like an affable, gentle giant, picked up little Clara Susan (the diminutive 4'6", fifty-year-old, toothless "Char Woman") and spun her around in circles. The sight of her sweet, toothless smile made me grin, but seeing her feet dangling two feet off the ground made me burst out laughing! Meanwhile, a few feet away, Julianna, secure in the arms of Clarissa's good friend Joel Kelly, leaned back, laughing hysterically as she tried in vain to escape being tickled. Clarissa, just three days shy of her nineteenth birthday, was looking fondly at the two of them, laughing almost as hard as Julie. Caleb, ten days shy of his thirteenth birthday, was making his usual rounds, going from one demanded hug to another, being smothered in the love and attention of what seemed like every man, woman, and child. Oh! Did I forget to mention the *girls* in that crowd of admirers? The girls loved him most of all—from the seven-year-old "Little Fan" to the twenty-year-old ushers to the sixty-year-old "Laundress"—*everybody* loved Caleb!

A few feet away, Cheryl smiled graciously as the director, John Sweeney, thanked her profusely for sacrificing so much and for sharing us (Clarissa, Caleb, and me) with him and so many others during the Christmas season. Knowing we had previously endured many hardships, he felt that our unusual history had allowed us to touch many peoples' hearts in a very special way. He knew how much Cheryl loved us, how important holiday traditions and family were to her, and how great a sacrifice it had been for us to be apart so much during the holidays. For a moment it somehow seemed to ease the sharpness of her pain to know that it was recognized. Oh, how happy Cheryl was that it was finally over! How happy we all were!

I stopped for a moment to thank Gayle Castleton, who had played Mrs. Cratchit, for the marvelous job she had done on stage and for a very special kindness she had shown us a few weeks earlier when she'd given Ian and me a pair of extra tickets to the BYU-Utah rivalry football game at Rice-Eccles Stadium. It turned out to be one of the greatest games I had ever seen—and one of the most memorable moments I would ever share with my son.

Gayle couldn't help laughing as she remembered Ian that afternoon. In a stadium full of Utes, a sea of red, Ian was courageously decked out in his blue-and-white Cougar paraphernalia. He wore a white BYU football sweatshirt I had originally bought for his mom, a BYU helmet from a Halloween costume he had worn when he was six, and a BYU flag draped over his shoulders like a cape. Seeing him in the midst of all those die-hard Ute fans, people might have questioned his *sanity*, but he certainly left no doubt as to his *allegiance*!

Ian's early elation from BYU's first quarter lead seemed to fade with each consecutive score by the Utes. By halftime he was a total wreck. Too stressed to talk, he just stared blankly forward in silence, even after I brought back a massive pile of food from the concession stand. For my son, the human vacuum cleaner, to ignore food, I knew he had to be really stressed!

Though Gayle and her family were Crimson Club members and die-hard Utah fans, she recalled how they couldn't help but be amused by the sudden and dramatic return of Ian's typical beaming smile and easy laughter when, on the last play of the game, BYU's quarterback, John Beck, threw to tight end Jonny Harline, who was completely unguarded in the end zone, for a game-winning touchdown.

Like all the Cougar fans, Ian and I could hardly handle the euphoria as the team mobbed Harline in the end zone! We laughed and hugged, then just stood there in awe for quite a while, surrounded by a lot of shocked, devastated, yet very polite and even complimentary Utah fans. On that day it almost didn't matter if you were a Ute or a Cougar. BYU won, but it had been such a great game that there really wasn't a loser. It was one of those rare occasions when everyone, regardless of their allegiance, could walk away from the stadium grateful to be able to say they had been there. (Of course, I probably only felt that way because my team won.)

Gayle and I laughed heartily as we shared our memories. I thanked her again and turned to leave. On my way from the rehearsal room to the hallway, I devoured a few more meatballs and chugged another glass or two of peach punch. At the door I gave the producers, Mark and Sally Dietlein, one last hug then caught up with the rest of my family and headed to the back of the theater to hold the door for my wife and daughters. We spoke for a couple of minutes with James Patee, the security guard, then made our way outside. Although the car was only twenty feet from the door, we somehow managed to say yet a half dozen more good-byes, give a few more hugs, and leave a few final warm holiday wishes. Then, with a deep sense of accomplishment and relief, I heaved a happy sigh as we all began to nestle into our car. As I held the door for Cheryl, I noticed she was shivering, so I took off my leather jacket and helped her put it on. She looked at me and smiled. Seeing how exhausted I was from an emotionally draining day, she had offered to drive home. That was how our relationship had been from the beginning. Hundreds and thousands of simple selfless acts of love had made our marriage a joy. Sensitivity to each other's feelings was a part of everyday life for us, but this simple act of offering to drive home would drastically alter each of our lives forever.

After closing Cheryl's door for her, I walked around to the passenger side of our old Mercury Sable and climbed in. With a deep breath and an enormous sigh, I let a thousand cares, a thousand stresses, and fifty performances slip gently away. We would finally be able to enjoy Christmas.

The winter chill and a slight fog had left a beautiful frosty glitter on both the car and the road. Everything looked so magical. The roads were nearly empty as we turned onto 35th South, headed a few blocks west, and eased our way up the I-215 on-ramp to head home to Cedar Hills.

Despite their excitement, the children were so worn out that, from the youngest to the oldest, they were already nodding off to sleep. It had been such a busy day and such an emotional one that it was little wonder they were all exhausted.

Rest seemed to come to all of us quickly and easily, and rightly so. I glanced at my sweet wife as she silently and selflessly drove, then looked at each of our sleeping children and smiled. I was surrounded by the people I loved most in the world. In the stillness of that peaceful night, life was as sweet as it had ever been. I was so grateful to be with my family.

# 3
## One Last Stop

CHERYL RELUCTANTLY AGREED TO MAKE one last stop on our way home. You see, Christmas still held all of its magic for most of the children but especially for our little Julianna. I wanted so badly to preserve that for at least one more year, and I felt like we needed just a few more things to make it magical.

How I regret that thought now!

As we pulled into Walmart's parking lot, it was Saturday night at 11:45. I glanced sheepishly at Cheryl and assured her that I would try to be in and out within fifteen minutes. After all, we didn't believe in shopping on Sundays.

Ian decided to run into the bathroom, so he got out of the car at the same time I did. As he came up and hugged me, it felt like he towered over me. Though only 5'11", a modest height in most circles, in my little hobbit-like household, he looked like Gandolph walking around the Shire. Still, I could never look at him without seeing the little two-year-old boy with the infectious smile, sitting on the kitchen counter covered in flour. As big as he had grown, he was still my "little buddy."

Ian and I did everything together. I taught him to draw then watched over the years as he created the most amazing cartoons I had ever seen. I taught him a few things about composing then sat back and marveled as he began writing beautiful music. He was such a blessing!

As we each closed our car door and started toward the store, Ian looked at me with a mischievous little grin and said, "Hey, Dad, I'll race you . . ."

I smiled. We had raced a thousand times. Once in a while we would take breaks from the football games that he, Caleb, and I played almost every day in our yard to run sprints against each other. Sometimes we would walk up the street to the golf course by our house and work on plyometric exercises to improve his speed. Ian wanted to get fast enough to play tight end at Lone Peak—and maybe someday at BYU.

Obviously, I'm not exactly at my best at 11:45 at night, especially after an exhausting day, and I'm worse in a slippery parking lot, but I've never been one to back down from a challenge. Besides, Ian had never beaten me, so I smiled back at him confidently and said, "You're on!"

As we zipped past the cars and eventually rounded the corner for the final stretch to the door, something shocking happened: he pulled ahead. By the time we cruised through the first set of doors, Ian was a good three yards in front of me! We were both astonished and so excited! He had achieved one of his toughest goals by improving his speed, and I had achieved one of mine by helping him do it. It was a dream come true for a father. He had not only become better than he used to be, he had become better than *me*. We were both so proud of him and so happy and so grateful that we grabbed each other and spun around, laughing and hugging. For a few moments, it was like time stood still and there was only us. I felt like Apollo Creed after he raced Rocky Balboa along the beach. When the student defeated his mentor, they hugged each other and splashed around in the waves, celebrating.

As I headed to the back of the store to pick up a few stocking stuffers and last-minute presents, Ian headed for the restrooms at the front. As we were about to part ways, he tapped me on the shoulder, turned me back around, gave me a huge bear hug, and said, "I love you, Dad."

I'm so thankful he did because those were the last words I would ever hear him say.

Fifteen minutes came and went, and I found myself still frantically rushing from one end of the store to the other. Realizing that, with the long lines, I couldn't possibly get out by midnight even if I left right then, I figured I might as well turn my attention toward trying to make every detail of Christmas as special as I could.

It's funny how time moves at such a different rate when you're in a store shopping than it does when you're in a car waiting for someone who's shopping. Twenty minutes in a large store is barely enough time to track down a few simple things, let alone check out in the middle of a mad Christmas rush—but it seems like an eternity when you're the one waiting in the car. This time it was even worse. Because the heater in our car was having some kind of problem, the only way Cheryl could keep everyone warm was to keep the car moving, so she drove up and down the rows of the parking lot the whole time she was waiting. Every now and then one of us would text the other for updates. After a long while, she texted me to ask where I was. I told her I was waiting in the check-out line. Twenty minutes later, when I *still* wasn't through the long, slow-moving line, she sent me a text: *I hope you can find a ride. I'm leaving.*

I called her a few minutes later to tell her I was finally swiping my debit card. After a brief, pleasant conversation, she said, "I love you, sweetie." She had ended our calls like that a million times before, but this time I appreciated it much more. She had reluctantly sent me into a store for fifteen short minutes only to endure driving in countless monotonous circles around a parking lot while she waited *much* longer. She had every right to lambast me, but even after all that, she still answered me with the same sweet kindness she always did. How grateful I was then and am now for that kindness, for those were some of the last words I ever heard her say.

When I finally made it back out to the car, I found that, in order to be more comfortable, everyone had changed seats. After racing me into the store, Ian had gone back to the car and taken my spot on the passenger side of the front seat. Julie had moved up to the middle of that seat to snuggle with her mom. Caleb had moved behind the driver's seat, where Ian would have been, so Clarissa could stretch out all across the rear of the car.

When I finally came out of the store, I approached the car from behind. I knocked softly on the trunk, and Cheryl pushed the button to pop it open. After cramming my purchases in and covering them up, I walked around to my door. As I reached for the handle to get in, I noticed that Ian was asleep in my spot. His face was so peaceful that I couldn't bear to wake him and make him move. I walked around to the driver's side and opened the back door. There I found Caleb, with Clarissa's legs on top of him.

"I have nowhere to sit," I said, hinting for them to move. Not surprisingly, not a sympathetic word was said.

As I gently began to slide Clarissa's feet out of the way so I could sit down, she sat up, Caleb slid over, and I squeezed into the backseat behind Cheryl. She drove around the recently reconfigured parking lot for a few minutes trying to find the way back to I-215 so we could go home. There was an obscure little exit beside the store, but she never found it. Exhausted, she eventually gave up and decided to go out the exit that she *could* see. We would just head home a different way. She turned onto 5300 South and started to make her way east toward I-15.

I had been so worried that Christmas wouldn't be as magical as we hoped. Now, at last, I could be completely at peace. Like everyone else, I was excited to get home so we could all rest. But I was grateful we had been able to make one last stop.

# 4
## I Never Heard a Sound

As we drove about ten blocks east, an occasional pothole startled me into lifting my head and looking around. After a few minutes, we eased to a gentle stop at a red light at 5300 South and 700 West. I opened my eyes and glanced around the car. I could see the freeway just ahead. Except for Cheryl and me, everyone was asleep. I looked lovingly at the children. I had just knelt at the grave of Tiny Tim and was reminded of the little ones we had buried over the years. My heart swelled with gratitude for the four of our nine who were still with us. I couldn't help but think of the story, *The Night Before Christmas*. As they all slept, so sweetly and peacefully, I smiled and imagined each one of them with "visions of sugarplums"[33] dancing in their heads.

I reflected on our struggles from Christmas the year before. After being forced to sell nearly everything, including both the house we lived in and the dream home we had built, as well as several businesses, then going eleven months without work, we had gone from excited hopes of a high six-figure absentee income to being under so much financial stress that Christmas dinner and many of our presents had been left on our doorstep by anonymous donors. It had been a horrible time. Unlike the very public trials we had endured which had moved so many to pray for us, our financial trial was private, so we went through it alone and suffered in silence. Although I know it must sound odd to say so, it was far more difficult than anything we had suffered before. It was embarrassing, demoralizing, and humiliating. I had no problem with being humbled. Three of my best outfits were made of sackcloth and ashes, and I found pride to be loathsome in any one. It was much harder for me to feel that I was robbed of my dignity and self-respect. As I remembered the awful pain of that year before, it was so sweet to think that things were back to normal. Life was good. And Christmas would be like it always used to be.

The light turned green, and we started across the intersection to make our way to the freeway just ahead. Suddenly, out of the corner of my eye, I saw a red pickup truck come speeding toward the intersection from our right. As it came hurtling toward us, I thought, *What is this guy doing? He isn't stopping!*

I glanced up at the light to be sure it was green. Realizing there was no way to escape, Cheryl screamed and tried to protect Julie. Then time suddenly slowed down.

I watched in stunned horror as the truck raced through the red light, sped into the intersection, and with a horrible loud crash, violently slammed into the right side of our car. Cheryl flew against the window to her left, sending the car swerving across the median and into oncoming traffic on the westbound side of the road. As she careened off the window, she fell down off the right side of the steering wheel, apparently unconscious. As she did, the car squealed and jerked violently back to the right. Wildly, the front wheels, then the back ones, bounced over the concrete median again, tossing us around like rag dolls. Although she was unconscious, Cheryl's foot was still on the accelerator, so we continued, out of control, back across the three lanes of traffic on our side of the road then abruptly slammed into the curb and bounced up onto a grassy knoll in front of the Smith's grocery store, where we mercifully came to a stop. The thunderous sound of the collision echoed in the night for a moment, and then everything suddenly went silent.

A sharp pain shot up my legs. My chest felt as if it had just been walloped, full force, with a baseball bat. As time crawled to a near standstill, I felt as if my body was completely shutting down. For what was probably only a minute or so but felt like an eternity, I felt like I was suffocating. My heart felt like it totally stopped. As the seconds passed, I desperately struggled for breath and began to panic and feel like I was dying. Just at the moment when I felt I was about to slip out of consciousness, perhaps for good, I felt a strange sensation. It was as if somebody pounded me in the chest and somehow hit my body's "reset button." Starved for oxygen, I gasped as if I had just surfaced after spending two desperate and terrifying minutes underwater. The air came flooding into my lungs; my heart, which felt like it had missed thirty or forty beats, started pumping again.

My stomach was tensely cramping as if in a seemingly endless contraction, making my breathing even more labored. I was disoriented, short of breath, and in pain, but I suddenly no longer felt like I was dying.

Dazed and nauseous, I struggled for a moment to gather myself and come to my senses. I couldn't seem to shake the cobwebs from my head enough to form a coherent thought. Gradually, slowly, I became more and more aware of what was happening around me. As I did, I immediately started to worry that somebody might have gotten hurt. With my voice frail, uneasy, and faltering, I nervously called out to my wife, "Cheryl?"

Apprehensively, I listened and waited, but there was no response. Growing fearful and concerned, I pleaded again for an answer, this time a little louder, "Cheryl?"

Again, there was nothing—just deafening silence. Uneasily I called out once more in desperation, "CHERYL?!"

With all my heart, I prayed to hear her answer me. I listened intently as the seconds ticked mercilessly away, but I never heard a sound . . .

# 5
## The Kind of Girl I'd Like to Marry

I met Cheryl Lynne Smith in August of 1985 at a cul-de-sac dance in Provo, Utah. There was an outdoor party at sunset, just around the corner from "the Cottage" where I lived for a time while I was studying at BYU. Oddly enough, neither of us had planned on being there that night. Cheryl worked at Aspen Grove, a family camp near Sundance, up Provo Canyon. She just happened to be down in the valley that night, visiting a friend who lived in a four-plex two houses north of mine. I, meanwhile, had planned a fun date with an old friend I had run into at the bookstore, but at the last minute, she'd stood me up. I soon learned that sometimes, when the Lord denies us a blessing, it's because He wants to give us something even better. And sometimes it's literally just around the corner.

Discouraged that my date had fallen through and feeling a little mopey and disheartened, I walked around the corner to the cul-de-sac where the dance was being held. My smile seemed to return quickly when I noticed a girl I had long had my eye on. I thought she had it all. She was the ward Relief Society president—a really good girl from a pioneer family that had crossed the plains—who loved the gospel, the scriptures, and the Savior. She was pure, talented, pretty, soft-spoken, and kind. She even sewed her own clothes, baked her own bread, and made cookies from scratch—the whole nine yards. She would have been perfect for me had it not been for her one tiny flaw: she didn't *like* me!

Of course I was no expert on dating, but I did know that things usually work out a lot better when the person you love actually loves you back! I didn't want someone who would love me in *spite* of who I was; I was waiting to find someone who would love me *because* of who I was.

For several minutes I tried in vain to woo this girl. But no matter how hard I tried to convince her that I was a perfect blend of

Spencer W. Kimball and Fabio, in her eyes I was actually half Yoda and half Grandpa from the Munsters!

Anyway, as I stood there blathering, I happened to glance up and see Cheryl just as she was arriving at the dance. I was instantly smitten! As if in a scene from Rodgers and Hammerstein's *Cinderella*, I stopped my fruitless lobbying midsentence and stared. Abruptly abandoning the girl I had previously thought was so special, I walked purposefully toward the beautiful and mysterious young woman who had just arrived at the ball. As I walked with my starry-eyed gaze fixed on the captivating stranger who had just arrived, I pointed to Cheryl and said to myself, with absolute wonder in my voice, "*That* is the kind of girl I'd like to marry!"

Although I'm sure I left the Relief Society president thoroughly puzzled, to *me* the moment was life-altering, and the statement was prophetic.

I danced with Cheryl over and over that night, occasionally offering an insincere but polite apology for trying to keep her all to myself: "Maybe I should give the other guys a chance to dance with you. Tell you what . . . I'll give them ten seconds!" As soon as I could see that there was no one nearby, I would count as fast as I could, then dance with her again.

Finally, after hours of swing dancing and dozens of romantic slow songs, I walked her home, stopping briefly on my porch to grab my guitar and sing her a song I had written. Before saying good night, I asked her if we could go out the following day, and she excitedly agreed. In some ways the things we would discover about each other the next day would surprise us both. But in other ways, they simply confirmed to me what I had already felt—*That* is the kind of girl I'd like to marry!

# 6
## Uncommon Things in Common

WE ARRIVED IN DOWNTOWN PROVO about twenty minutes early for the movie *Ladyhawke*. That gave us an opportunity to go for a walk and get to know each other better. As we strolled, we talked about everything imaginable. With each new subject, we found we had more and more in common. It was strangely wonderful and wonderfully strange; I felt like I had found a really pretty female version of myself. But when the conversation turned to the subject of family, we each seemed to get a little bit sheepish.

At first glance Cheryl seemed to be one of those five-generation Mormon girls I thought were so wonderful. I was a convert from a part-member family (my father, who was raised a Moslem in Turkey, didn't convert when the rest of the family did). As I started to realize how pure and sweet Cheryl was and how deeply she loved the Lord—more than anyone I had ever met before—I started asking myself, *What would a girl like* her *want with a guy like* me, *who not only has skeletons in his family closet but strewn all over the front lawn?*

Little did I know, she was asking herself what a guy like me would want with a girl like her. Reluctantly, she shared with me that she was the only one in her family who was a member of the Church. She seemed surprised when I smiled at that instead of squirming. "My father isn't a member of the Church," she explained, staring at her shoes, "and when I was little he drank a lot."

I just sat and listened. She seemed relieved that I didn't write her off or just go running. Encouraged by my acceptance, she continued to share one thing after another that she thought might scare me off, until she finally got to the really big one. I could see that it was difficult for her to talk about. I gently put my hand on her shoulder and said, "It's okay."

She didn't know how or why, but she could feel that it really *was* okay. She gathered her courage then blurted out: "When I was thirteen, my mother left and ran off with my dad's best friend."

My chin dropped, and I stared at her in silence.

"I should have known that one would be too much for you," she said.

She looked sullenly down at her feet. Her sadness was heart-wrenching.

"I understand," I said.

"How could you possibly understand?" she asked. "No one can."

Filled with compassion, I looked into her eyes. "Let me tell you a story."

I told her of when *I* was thirteen. I'd sat and listened in disbelief as two of my older brothers, Dennis and Erol, informed my father that our mother had not been spending weekends at our grandmother's as she had said; she had gotten involved with another man. She had innocently responded to a question this man had posed in a newspaper article. He had spent twenty-seven of his thirty-eight years in boys' homes and prisons. Sitting in a jail cell, from which he had written three books, he mused, "If there is a God, why does He let us suffer?" Moved to compassion, she wrote to reassure the man, explaining that God sometimes tries us to test our faith to keep us in remembrance of Him and to help us to grow. The man wrote back, and the relationship slowly began to escalate from a simple testimony to letters of a different kind, then to screen visits and fifty-pound weekly food packages. Eventually the man was being released on special furloughs, and Mom, having been approved as a prison escort, was accompanying him.

As my brothers continued to pile up accusations, all I could do was sit there, dumbfounded. It was simply impossible for me to believe that my good mother could ever do what they were suggesting.

The truth is it sounded so crazy that Dad didn't believe it either. He knew she had always been a good and devout Christian woman.

"Your mother would never do that," he insisted.

Just as my father was assuring my brothers that Mom was too loving and loyal and good to ever do such a thing, she walked in the door from a weekend away. My father's love for and trust in my mother reassured me, so I was excited to have her come in and clear up the whole absurd misunderstanding. As she moved from the kitchen into the dining room,

Dad walked into the living room and picked up the scriptures from the end table next to our couch. Although he was never a practicing Moslem as an adult, he had been raised by an extremely devout mother, who had in fact been on the pilgrimage to Mecca *three times*. Although Dad hadn't joined The Church of Jesus Christ of Latter-day Saints when the rest of the family did, he knew how much the scriptures meant to us. Calmly, he took the Bible, the Book of Mormon, the Doctrine and Covenants, and the Pearl of Great Price, and he set them in the center of the dining room table. He placed her scriptures in front of her. "Edith," he said confidently, "I want you to put your hand on these scriptures and tell me nothing happened with that man."

I was as anxious as he was to hear her denial so we could put the whole silly thing to rest. As I expected, she answered quickly. What I didn't expect was the answer she gave. She just glared at my father angrily and snapped, "I don't have to swear; I'm not in court."

I could feel my father's heart sink as he fell back in his chair. I was disgusted, shocked, and devastated. I can't even begin to imagine what *he* felt; I was stunned, mortified, and in total disbelief.

As I pondered the gravity of the situation, I started to fear how my father, with his very different upbringing and fiery temper, might respond. Dad was raised by people who firmly believed in the adage "an eye for an eye and a tooth for a tooth." What's more, in his native culture, if a man spilled a drink at the dinner table, it was because his wife had put the glass in the wrong place. How on earth would he handle something like this?

My father never once hit me. Even so, whenever he got angry, he scared me half to death. I knew this was something a lot bigger than finding out that we had thrown a baseball through our neighbor's basement window or that we had been hiding a kitten in the basement for two weeks, and I *knew* how upset he had gotten over *those* things! I was terrified and tried to brace myself for whatever might come next, but I could never have prepared myself for what actually happened. His response would change my life forever.

Dad clenched his jaw and put the side of his pointer finger in front of his lips like he always did when he was angry, then he started to shake his head in frustration.

*Here it comes,* I thought.

He paused for a moment, took a deep breath to gather himself, and uttered this unforgettable phrase, "If you come back and stay with me, and promise to never see him again, I will act as if nothing ever happened."

I couldn't believe what I was hearing! Such a gesture by *any* man would have been amazing, but for someone like my father, it was nothing short of a miracle! I had never seen such an incredible example of Christlike forgiveness! And yet it came from a man who wasn't even a Christian! His mercy, however, was tempered with justice. He explained her other choice. "Otherwise, get out!"

As heartbroken as I was that my mother, of all people, could have done anything like she had, I was even more floored by my father's remarkable response. What an incredible gesture of mercy! I was so grateful for it. I realized that his one simple act of forgiveness could keep our family together. She obviously couldn't turn down an offer like that, so I spun around on my chair to watch her take the simple oath. When I turned to look at her, she was no longer behind me. Seething, she'd stormed off into the bedroom. I followed her then watched in horror and tears as she silently packed her things and left.

No one can begin to describe the feelings of a thirteen-year-old, who, in a few brief moments, is confronted first with a mother's infidelity and then with her leaving forever. She was *abandoning* everything that mattered—her home, her husband, her family, her church, and *me*—temporarily deceived into thinking that something else was more important. I could not describe in a million years what I felt as I watched her leave. Even if I could, how could anyone ever understand it?

As I finished my sad tale, I looked at Cheryl to see her response. Tears of compassion and *empathy* were streaming down her face. I realized that she *did* understand, for she had known the same heartache herself.

From that moment on, we began to discover that we shared similar feelings and opinions about virtually *everything*, from politics to our taste in food, music, and movies; from our troubled pasts to our idealistic dreams; and from our desire to have children to our feelings about how we wanted to raise and discipline them. More than anything else, we each wanted to raise a family to the Lord.

Eventually we determined to do it together.

On December 13, 1985, Cheryl and I sealed our love for time and all eternity in the Salt Lake Temple and began a beautiful life of joy and selfless love, both of which would be nurtured, proven, and perfected through years of grand blessings and intense trials. Together we would learn to accept each graciously. We knew we could make it through anything if we stuck together, and we were both committed to being together forever.

Now, as I stared at Cheryl, who lay motionless in the seat in front of me, memories of the twenty-one years of marriage we had celebrated just eleven days earlier filled my heart with unspeakable gratitude and the heart-piercing loneliness that she and our precious children had helped me to forget. Father in Heaven, knowing the longings and pleadings of two of His precious children, had allowed us to answer each other's prayers and our sadness to be swept away in a flood of acceptance and love.

I treasure the moment when we were suddenly no longer strangers to each other but to loneliness!

I once wrote Cheryl, saying: *Life with you, so effortless and full of joy, makes it hard for me to remember, or even believe that once upon a time I couldn't even imagine a life as sweet as ours. The happiness you bring me was but an elusive dream for me until there was you!*

I couldn't bear the thought of losing that happiness or that wonderful woman with whom I had so many uncommon things in common.

# 7
## All We Ever Wanted

It was beautiful to love someone so completely and to be loved so warmly and unconditionally in return. I began to realize what a rare gift that truly was, for it was one that many people around me—both single and married—were not blessed to enjoy. Cheryl helped me to discover a kind of closeness and caring that was different from and far beyond anything I had ever known before.

We considered ourselves idealistic; others thought we were naïve. For example, we wanted to have as many children as we possibly could; we wanted to discipline them without spanking; and we wanted our home to be a place that was so full of love and harmony that nobody ever raised their voice unless the house was on fire. Most people scoffed at the idea, saying it was not only corny but unrealistic. They told us we were living in a dream world. Even so, we somehow managed to do it anyway.

Sometimes I would tell my brother Erol how happy I was or how easy it was to be married to Cheryl. He would roll his eyes and say, "The only reason you two are so happy is you're both too stupid to realize how miserable you should be."

They do say ignorance is bliss. We just figured that even if he was right, it was better to be delusional, dumb, and happy than realistic, smart, and miserable.

Cheryl and I both wanted to love as Jesus did. For her that came naturally. I had to work a little harder at it. I tried to pay special attention to people like Cheryl, who already *were* what I was hoping to someday become, and then imitate them. My hope was that if I could discipline myself to act selflessly, even when it seemed to be contrary to my nature, eventually it could *become* my nature. I tried to focus on meeting my wife's needs instead of my own. It was easy to do because I knew I could trust her to do the same for me. Seeking each other's happiness before our own allowed us to begin to understand the amazing selfless love of the Savior. Marriage seemed effortless and wonderful, and I often told Cheryl so. I once wrote: *Whenever I am stirred by a sunset; when moonlight silhouettes the mountains and transforms the dancing city lights into a magical sea that glistens until it gently disappears into the yellow dawn; when majestic French horns or crying violins speak peace to my weary soul; when I just can't wait to tell someone what I did that day, what I saw, what I learned, what I felt; when music or scenery or life is just too beautiful to enjoy alone, just knowing that you are near me and that you love the things I love heightens my joy and makes me grateful that God, in His wisdom and love, made us one.*

We tried hard to make sure that every decision we made contributed to oneness and made us closer. That effort, combined with Cheryl's natural disposition to be a peacemaker, blessed our home with a sweet and gentle spirit from the very beginning. We were *so* grateful for each other and so eager to live our dream of raising a family of faith. All we lacked were the children to be able to fulfill it.

When we first got married, I was already twenty-four and about to graduate from BYU with a degree in finance; Cheryl was twenty-six. We had both been taught that if a couple wasn't ready to have children, they weren't ready to get married and that those who curtailed the birth of children for selfish reasons would reap disappointment in the end, so for us family planning meant "planning to have a family." We hoped for a honeymoon baby but soon learned that it was not meant to be. Month after month we prayed for a child. After more than a year of marriage, the blessing we longed for so much and prayed for so fervently had still not come. We began to worry that something might be wrong. We were immensely happy together and grateful for all we had, but we still lamented what we did *not* have, namely, children.

While many young married couples were postponing marriage and childbearing in order to get degrees, buy larger homes, travel the world, or "establish themselves," we were fasting and praying to have a baby. And while all the "normal people" were using contraceptives or even abortion to be sure they *didn't* have children, we were trying everything we could to make sure we *did*. We considered it a privilege to be partners with God in bringing children into the world. Like most couples who wait in vain to be blessed with children, we shed many private tears as we wondered what was wrong with us.

We tried to listen cheerfully to all the talks and lessons on how to teach the children we longed to have, but it hurt to be reminded that we still didn't have them. Sometimes it was a struggle to hide our pain. On fast Sundays, Cheryl would fight back tears as one family after another blessed a newborn baby. She would cringe whenever someone joked about all the births in the ward, saying, "There must be something in the water." Somehow, no matter how much of that water we drank, and no matter what else we tried, we just couldn't seem to get pregnant. For someone like Cheryl who spent her youth dreaming of a family, approaching thirty with empty arms was heart-wrenching.

Eventually we were blessed with a pregnancy. How excited we were when that trial of waiting ended! As I think back on it now, hindsight almost makes our pain seem ridiculous, but as we struggled through it, not knowing if children would ever come to us, it was a source of tremendous heartache.

Although at the time it seemed like it might never end, our battle with infertility lasted "but a small moment."[34] I cannot imagine how painful and difficult it must be for those who know that longing for a *lifetime*! Still, that comparatively brief moment allowed the Lord to try our faith a little. We tried to prove that we would be willing to endure whatever He required to bring children into the world. As I reflect on the challenges Cheryl and I would face over the next several years, it is clear to me why it was so important for Him to do that.

Our hearts were so full of gratitude when, in the spring of 1987, we learned that the Lord would at last bless us with a child. All our lives that was all we ever wanted.

# 8
## Life Can Change in a Heartbeat

THE FIRST OF THOSE GREAT challenges would come sooner than we ever imagined. When Cheryl was about four and a half months into that first pregnancy, she had a craving one day for a chicken sandwich, so we drove to a restaurant a few miles from our house to get one. After enjoying our meal, we were ready to head home. As Cheryl scampered into the bathroom for one of her increasingly frequent "pit stops," I headed outside to get the car so she wouldn't have to walk very far. I pulled up next to the entrance and waited for her to come out, poised to spring out and open the door for her as soon as she appeared. After ten or fifteen minutes, she still hadn't come out. I started to get worried and finally decided that I had better go in and check on her. I slipped the gearshift into park, got out, and walked around the front of the car to the entrance. Just as I reached out to pull the long metal handle on the glass door, Cheryl appeared on the other side of it, drenched in blood from the waist down and sobbing inconsolably. It was obvious that she was hemorrhaging, and from her tears I could tell she had lost the baby.

"Oh, honey!" I exclaimed, rushing in to help her. She couldn't say a word. All she could do was cry.

As I helped her to the car and tried to comfort her, she was overcome by a barrage of emotions, including a dozen kinds of regret. She blamed herself for not eating better and condemned herself for having a "messed-up body" that "couldn't even carry a baby." My heart ached for the loss of our child, but it hurt even more for her.

With no choice but to resign myself to the shocking truth that we had just lost our baby, my only immediate concern was for my wife. Customers looked on with compassion and concern, some of them crying as we were, while employees hurried over to see if there was anything they could do to help. I closed Cheryl's car door and sped off to her obstetrician's office, hoping he would know what to do to stop the bleeding. Thankfully, the office was just a few blocks away, so we arrived quickly. Seeing that it was an emergency, he took her right into one of the examination rooms. I recall my feeling as I sat beside her bed, holding her hand, trying so hard to be strong for her when inside my own heart was breaking. I whispered, "Everything will be okay. You're going to be fine."

But I think I was saying that to calm my own fears as much as hers.

The doctor told us it would be necessary to do a D&C. He tried to describe the procedure delicately, but it still sounded gruesome. Nevertheless, our concern for Cheryl's health overrode everything else, so we acquiesced and gave our consent. Within moments he started making all the necessary preparations. First he had to do an ultrasound to see how extensive the surgery would be.

Between intermittent whimpers, Cheryl just laid there, her eyes welling up with tears as they squeezed the cold, blue gel on her lower belly. She struggled to fight back memories of how they had done the very same thing just a few days earlier, announcing the gender and praising the growth of what they had then said was a perfectly healthy baby girl. My own sorrow and compassion overcame me, and we both cried uncontrollably.

The doctor rolled his chair toward the ultrasound monitor to examine the placenta. With a somewhat puzzled-looking grimace, he leaned forward and squinted to examine the image more closely. Clearly startled and alarmed by what he saw, he gasped and exclaimed, "Oh my!"

My heart sank.

*What now?* I wondered as I offered a quick silent prayer: *Dear Father in Heaven, have mercy on us! I don't think we can handle any more bad news. And* please *don't let there be anything wrong with Cheryl!*

Without a word, the doctor continued to stare at the image trying to confirm what he thought he saw. The longer he stared, the more worried I felt. Finally he looked at me, raised his eyebrows, and answered, "There's a *heartbeat!*"

Shocked by his statement, Cheryl, her nurse, and I all quickly turned to look at him, sure that we must have all heard wrong. The doctor shrugged his shoulders, showing that he didn't understand it himself. Then he put his hand on Cheryl's shoulder, warmly smiled, and repeated excitedly, "There's a heartbeat!"

Our baby was still *alive*!

In an instant the greatest sorrow we had ever known was transformed into the greatest joy, and our hearts swelled with inexpressible gratitude for a totally unexpected and almost unimaginable miracle.

The Lord taught us a principle then that our life experiences would later confirm many times in the coming years: joy and sorrow are two sides of the same coin. The pain and heartache that come from life's trials, whatever they may be, create in us a greater depth of feeling. Suffering stretches our souls and increases our capacity to feel. In the very moment that God allowed us to experience extraordinary pain, grief, and sorrow, He enabled us to receive more perfect comfort, unspeakable joy, and incomprehensible peace.

Eventually the doctor sent us home with a hope that had risen, like a phoenix, out of death and ashes.

Cheryl was ordered to strict bed rest for an extended period of time. It was my responsibility—and *honor* and *pleasure*—to wait on and care for her and our unborn child. For months I prepared all of our meals, cleaned the house, did the laundry, read stories to her, and even changed her bedpans. I felt it a privilege to do anything I could to make her comfortable and allow her to rest, in the hope that we could save our little one.

During those months of service, I began to understand the type of love that my parents—both on earth and in heaven—had for me, and I came to appreciate the kind of adoration and service I was duty-bound to offer in return. I realized that because I loved my wife and baby so much, I was willing to do *anything* for them. Nothing brought me more joy than to serve them and make them happy. By extension, I came to understand more clearly how I was meant to serve the Lord—not out of some feeble fear of punishment, nor a pathetically selfish desire for some kind of reward, but simply because I wanted to please the one I loved so much!

Cheryl would recover enough over the next couple of months for us to go on what we would later call our *wandering in the wilderness.* With the thought of being closer to family, we decided to move across the country to Washington, D.C. I was actually pounding the For Sale by Owner sign into our front yard when someone drove up and made us an offer.

A few days later we loaded a twenty-six foot truck and, with eighty-five references of BYU alumni in hire-and-fire positions and a naïve sense of hopeful optimism, we drove back East to look for work. Over the course of the next six weeks, we were never able to contact a single one of those references. It seemed like every door was closed and every road was blocked.

After a few days, we were forced to put our things in storage. We were living in hotels and eating in restaurants, and the money we made on the sale of our home was disappearing rapidly. Confused and discouraged, we decided I would apply for a position at Merrill Lynch in New York, where I had worked in commodity research in 1980 and 1981 before serving as a missionary in Chile. My brother Erol's wife, Jenny, now the corporate treasurer of eBay, was just vacating a position there. When I interviewed for the job, I had the benefit of her recommendation, that of one of the vice presidents, and those of several others I had worked with previously, as well as a familiarity with many of the processes, systems, and people associated with the job. My interview went fabulously well. I had so much going for me, and it seemed like I had found a perfect fit. Even so, I wasn't called back for a second interview. In despair I lamented to Cheryl, "If I can't get *that* job, I can't get *any* job here!"

Disillusioned by the dirty environment and wanting to live close to a temple, we headed back to Virginia. After several more weeks of searching, we were ready to give up. That always seems to be the Lord's cue.

After spending thousands of dollars on living expenses, I said, "I'm not going to pay for another night in a hotel!"

I was determined to spend the night in the car. I parked behind a Holiday Inn. It was about 95 degrees with 95 percent humidity. We opened the windows, reclined our seats, and tried to get some rest. I glanced over at Cheryl. There she sat, seven months' pregnant, staring out the window, totally despondent. My heart ached for her. She had put her faith in me, and I was letting her down. I tried to lighten the mood. I grinned and joked, "At least it isn't raining."

No sooner had I said the words than with a flash of lighting and a roar of thunder, it started to pour. Whatever mascara hadn't already been dripping down her face from the tears was now running off in the rain. It was such a pathetic sight! I made one last feeble attempt at optimism: "It could always be worse . . ."

Cheryl just stared at me in disgust, as if to say, *Oh, really? By all means, enlighten me.*

My mind raced desperately to think of anything positive to say. Finally, I blurted out, "Well, at least the . . . hotel isn't . . . on fire."

Heavenly Father, with His divine sense of humor, must have overheard, because not ten seconds later the fire alarm in the hotel went off, and they had to evacuate the building. Cheryl and I looked at each other and began to laugh hysterically. We laughed all the way to the Comfort Inn down the street, where we checked in for the night.

The next morning I woke up and made an amazingly insightful observation: "I'm beginning to think that maybe the Lord wants us someplace else." You can imagine how dazzled Cheryl was by my unparalleled perceptivity.

We spent the next several hours talking about where we really wanted to be. We both wanted to be back "home" in Utah. The question was, where could I work? I thought back to the day we had our engagement photos taken. We were standing by the runnels outside the Church Office Building, having our picture taken with the Salt Lake Temple in the background. As the sun set, I held Cheryl in that incredibly romantic setting, looked up at the Church Office Building, and said, "I'm going to work there someday."

Unemployed, sitting in a hotel room in Virginia, I thought the idea sounded better than ever. The only problem was, I was two thousand miles away, and I had absolutely no idea what they even *did* in that building. I decided there was only one way to find out—I called. I asked what kind of qualifications I would need to work there.

"I don't suppose you speak Spanish by any chance, do you?" the voice on the other end asked.

"Yes, I actually do. I was a missionary in Chile."

She asked me if I could wait a minute; then she put me on hold. When she returned she asked, "Do you think you could come in for an interview at ten o'clock tomorrow morning?"

I couldn't believe my ears. Without even thinking, I told her I could. She thanked me for calling and said good-bye. I immediately turned to my wife and told her what happened. She nearly put herself into labor bouncing up and down on the bed in excitement.

"But I can't fly all the way back there just for one silly interview!" I told her.

Then I got an ingenious idea. I decided to call the man at BYU who had given me the eighty-five bogus references that had put me in this predicament in the first place. I pulled his business card from my wallet, dialed his number, and explained our situation.

"You owe me big time," I told him.

He started laughing, but *I* didn't. I was dead serious. I had just been on a six-week-long wild goose chase that had cost me thousands of dollars. "I want you to get me an interview for a financial position in Salt Lake . . . *tomorrow*."

He told me he would do his best then hung up. A half hour later, he called me back to say he had arranged an interview for me with Wells Fargo at two in the afternoon.

I immediately set about trying to book a flight. After hours of checking with airlines and travel agents, the best I could do was $1,699 round trip.

"I can't spend that much. What if it turns out to be a giant waste of time?" I asked.

We decided to kneel down and pray. We poured out our hearts to the Lord, pleading that He would help us to know the right thing to do. We asked him to either provide the way or provide a roadblock.

For several hours we continued to make phone calls to every travel agent and airline we could find numbers for—with no luck. Around half past five, we had spoken to one agent who said she was swamped but would try to check for us, but she had never called back. Finally, at six o'clock, the last travel agency closed. And at quarter after six, we gave up all hope of hearing from her. It seemed that we had apparently gotten the roadblock. We were so disheartened!

Just then the telephone rang. It was the travel agent we had spoken to earlier. Excitedly, she told us, "The strangest thing happened. Just a few minutes ago, after we were supposed to be closed, somebody called and cancelled. I can get you a ticket for $299 round trip."

The moment we heard those words, we knew I was going to get that job. I interviewed with eleven people in the Church Office Building the next day (as well as the one at Wells Fargo) before flying back to be with Cheryl. Once we were together again, we drove up to my mother's place in New Jersey to spend the weekend. On Monday morning, someone from the Church offices called and offered me the job. I would work there for the next seventeen years.

Within a few days, we were using up the last of our money to get our things out of storage, reload them on a twenty-six-foot truck, and drive them across the country to a new home just thirty miles away from where we started!

Cheryl eventually went into labor the day after Christmas, on December 26, 1987. Perhaps she and I should have gone for that long walk on Christmas *Eve* instead of Christmas *Day*! What a sweet and memorable Christmas that was! With Cheryl pregnant and my bearded older brother, Dennis, in town, it made for the most authentic little nativity reenactment we'd ever had.

Cheryl's labor was relatively short (of course that's easy for *me* to say)—just an hour and a half. All of those Lamaze classes and our prepacked suitcase with everything from tennis balls and soothing music to slippers and rolling pins really paid off. Caring more about the health of the baby than her own comfort, my wife decided to deliver our daughter naturally, without any pain medication. It was humbling to see how love could motivate someone to willingly endure such incredible pain.

We waited anxiously to pass each of the emotional signposts we were told would clearly indicate when she was finally in transition. It was obvious when they came.

"*Ice chips!*" Cheryl blurted out, without the usual "Honey, could I please have . . ." that would have preceded her request just fifteen minutes earlier. I hurriedly dipped a plastic spoon into the Styrofoam cup on the nightstand and, in seconds, held the ice to her parched lips. "No! No! No! Get those things out of here!"

I looked up at the nurse-midwife, bewildered. Without a word she consoled me with a knowing grin.

Then came the telltale sign; my normally sweet wife glared at me and snapped, "YOU DID THIS TO ME!"

Well, you get the idea. She was in transition all right!

Despite the uncharacteristic abuse—for which she would later apologize profusely—I was excited because I knew what was coming next . . . a baby! Three pushes later Cheryl gave birth to a beautiful baby girl. In one magical moment, I became a proud papa, and Cheryl was transformed into the noblest of all of God's creations—a mother!

We named our daughter "Clarissa" after the adorable little blonde girl in the movie *Mr. Krueger's Christmas*, who inadvertently left one of her mittens at the old man's house. When she and her mother returned to look for it, they discovered he had hung it as the lone ornament on his tiny tree because the girl reminded him of everything good about Christmas. That's exactly how we felt about *our* Clarissa. Her name also brought back fond memories of "Clarisse," Rudolph the Red-Nosed Reindeer's soft-spoken girlfriend who sang the song "There's Always Tomorrow" (for dreams to come true). Clarissa's middle name was Nicole, after good old Saint Nick.

I have always seen our daughter Clarissa's birth as a special blessing. When she was conceived, she was our first miracle; when she was spared, she was our second; and when she finally came home, she was our third. Each tug we felt on our heartstrings throughout the ordeal—from our longing to have her, to her time in intensive care for jaundice, to our happy arrival home—helped prepare us for the next great challenge that was soon to follow.

That Christmas, Cheryl gave me the most wonderful gift imaginable, the first gift of Christmas—a child! From that beginning and the joy and wonder that each successive child would add, Christmas would forever be our most treasured time of year.

I learned something when we nearly lost Clarissa that our accident would confirm nearly two decades later—life can change in a heartbeat.

# 9
## Crushed

THE BLARING SOUND OF PIERCING sirens brought me back to the present. As those sirens wailed in the distance, Clarissa wailed even louder just a few feet away. When I heard her bloodcurdling screams as she tried in vain to move, I glanced over to where she sat, contorted and grimacing, on the other side of Caleb. She was writhing in pain, panicked, and restlessly squirming, either to free herself or to try to find a position to relieve her suffering. Exhausted from struggling, she would periodically lay her head on the back dash and close her eyes as she tried to gather strength to fight some more. With Ian's seat reclined and her side of the car smashed in, I couldn't see her legs and began to wonder if she even still had them. I had watched my beautiful daughter dance and perform from the time she was three years old. Now almost nineteen and having just finished her first semester at BYU, she had been excitedly anticipating the upcoming auditions for the school's world-renowned international folk-dance team. Her door had taken half of the impact of the truck, blasting the middle third of her back several inches out of alignment. Her legs were trapped in hot, twisted metal, and she couldn't move from the waist down.

The whole right side of our Sable, from wheel well to wheel well, had been pushed into the middle of the car as if it were part of a giant collapsing accordion. In addition, we had been hit so hard that the bottom of the car had curled up over the side. Everything seemed to be crushed—our car; our daughter's legs, which I could not even see for all the twisted metal; and, with her legs, her dreams of becoming a dancer.

As I looked around in horror, I found that the scope and terrible consequences of the accident were growing more and more grim with each passing second. As the awful realities continued to unfold and our losses continued to mount, I began to feel overwhelmed. I suddenly realized that, like everything around me, I too felt crushed.

# 10
## Two of My Best Friends

IN TERROR I QUICKLY LOOKED around in an effort to set up a sort of mental triage. Looking down to my right, I found Ian lying on the floor by my foot. I thought back to when I first got back to the car after shopping.

I guess he knew me well enough to figure I would take a while in the store. Like Cheryl, he had waited for me more than a time or two before. It seemed as if he had been planning on me taking a long time because when I finally got back to the car, he was up front on the passenger side in the larger, more comfortable bucket seat. As I had approached the car, I saw him reclining in the bucket seat, all sprawled out and sleeping like a baby.

But now, dazed from the crash and perhaps subconsciously trying to block out the painful truth of what had actually happened, I wondered how he got to my feet. It wasn't until months later that my mind would allow me to remember more of the details of the moment we got hit. Eventually I was able to replay in my mind the part of the accident I had blocked out. As if in some bizarre slow-motion flashback, I saw Ian the moment the truck hit his door. Thrown violently out of his seat, his head slammed into my knee, forcing my legs to smack into each other. Then he slid off my knee, down my leg, and to the floor with a thud.

He lay there unconscious, almost completely facedown, his shoulders facing me only slightly. He made no sound and remained totally unresponsive as I carefully lifted him up, gently rested his head between my lap and Caleb's. I immediately began to give him a blessing. Some of what happened then is too sacred to share. What I can say is that just as I began to speak, Ian had some sort of horrible hemorrhage. A massive amount of blood came flooding from his nose in one enormous, horrifying gush. Suddenly drenched in my son's blood, I started to panic.

I was overwhelmed and terrified. I had no idea what could cause such a thing or what I could to do to help him. The only thing I could think to do was lay my fingers on his neck to check for a pulse.

There was none.

Ian had gone to sleep dreaming of Christ's birth. Moments later, he would awake to the reality of His Resurrection.

I was too much in shock to even cry. In disbelief, I gently laid his head back down on my lap and stared blankly at him, stroking his hair. I was only beginning to comprehend the horror of what was actually happening.

Once again, my mind began racing. My thoughts wandered from the accident to dozens of experiences that I suddenly felt had been preparing me for this. As thousands of memories flooded my mind, I thought about Cheryl. It broke my heart to think about how hard it would be for her to learn that we had lost another child.

I glanced up at her, lying slumped over in the front seat. She still hadn't moved. For a moment I stared at her back to see if I could notice her breathing. She was totally still. For the first time, it occurred to me that this was so much worse than I had imagined.

Only a few minutes had passed since we had been hit, yet speeding fire engines, ambulances, and police cars were already appearing. Captain Joe Wilken and his partner, Paul Hare, from Salt Lake County's Unified Fire Authority were the first to arrive. Wearing full fireman's regalia, they rushed to the car to help. I remember vividly when they arrived and peered into the windows from either side of the car. Wilken glanced at Ian for only an instant then looked up at his partner. I will never forget the look on his face as, with his eyes alone, he tacitly told his companion, *This one is gone.* Paul Hare quickly checked Cheryl then stared at his captain and very slightly shook his head side to side, as if to say, *So is this one.* My heart sank.

In the midst of terror and triage, I learned I had lost two of my best friends.

# 11
## Chosen

IAN WAS TRULY EXTRAORDINARY. HE had already grown to be a man in many ways, but in his tall, strong body, he still had the tender, teachable heart and sweet innocence of a child. He loved the Savior and tried hard to be like Him. Overall, Ian became the same kind of man his hero was. Beside his bed hung a poster of Captain Moroni, a military and spiritual leader in the Book of Mormon. What was said of Moroni might also be said of Ian: "If all men had been and were, and ever would be like unto [him], the very powers of hell would have been shaken forever, yea the devil never would have power over the hearts of the children of men."[35]

Part of the reason we always had such a great relationship—and why Ian had always meant so much to me—was because he was the first of my sons who lived past infancy.

After almost losing Clarissa, Cheryl gave birth to three children in a row who lived less than three weeks.

The first tragedy struck in 1988 when Clarissa was only ten months old. On the same day we learned we were going to have fraternal twins, a boy and a girl, Cheryl went into premature labor. Our excitement quickly turned to heartache. With their lungs still underdeveloped, our son Jordan Erol and our daughter Brianna Corrinne lived less than an hour. After what would prove to be her longest and hardest labor, Cheryl would leave the hospital with empty arms.

A year later, we learned we were going to have another son. We chose to give him the same name as his brother who had died. When Cheryl was about five months along in this pregnancy, we were told that our baby would be born with a birth defect called hydrocephalous, or water on the brain. The doctor told us that if our son was lucky enough to be in the 40 percent who survive the first year, he was likely to have a normal life-span, but he would have only a one in three chance of normal brain function. Some doctors insisted that we take the baby early or the hydrocephalous would compress his brain tissue and cause him to be mentally retarded, perhaps severely; others warned that we had to wait for his lungs to be developed or we would lose him as we had the twins. The months of waiting were torture, and every choice made us feel guilty.

There was a *slight* hope that our son would be able to lead a completely normal life, but the chances were very slim. A plan evolved. It was suggested that just after our son's birth, a neurosurgeon, Dr. Walker, would install "a shunt" (a thin rubber draining tube with a regulating valve). A half hour after delivery, Dr. Walker did a CT scan to determine how to place it. After looking closely at the scans, he came to the room where Cheryl was recovering from the C-section that had been required. He pulled up a chair beside Cheryl's bed, motioned for me to take a seat, then said, "You'd better sit down. I have some bad news."

When at last Jordan was born, we thought the trial was finally over. He looked fabulous! Dr. Walker would put in that shunt, and our son was going to be fine. Dr. Walker told us that he himself had had a shunt because he'd had hydrocephalous, so we had high hopes.

However, after doing the CT scan, Dr. Walker explained what he found. "Your son doesn't actually have congenital hydrocephalous," he began.

That didn't sound like bad news to me.

"The fluid is pooling because there's a blockage."

He could tell we didn't understand. He had no choice but to spell it out for us. His face got very serious, but I still wasn't ready when he said, "I'm afraid your son has a brain tumor."

Within hours Dr. Walker would be performing a difficult brain surgery. He hoped to do a biopsy to determine if the tumor was malignant or benign, then he would attempt to remove it. Unfortunately the surgery nearly took Jordan's life. He came out of it paralyzed, blind, and in a coma. He would only live for three weeks.

After losing three children in a row, our grief was unimaginable. After wading through so much sorrow, we could not begin to express the joy we felt when on January 26, 1991, Ian was born healthy. It was magnified a hundredfold! For, as the American poet Edwin Markham explained, "Only the soul that knows the mighty grief can know the mighty rapture. Sorrows come to stretch out spaces in the heart for joy."[36]

## *He Can Heal*

\*\*\*

For most of his life, Ian, like Clarissa, was homeschooled by his mom. Cheryl quickly discovered how to develop his natural curiosity into a passion for learning. As he grew, he seemed to run through a series of eccentric little obsessions. As a toddler, his very first passion was trucks. For a short time, it seemed to be all he would talk about. Later his interest shifted to things like rain forests and drawing. Instead of trying to force him to focus on what he was "supposed to" be learning, Cheryl would not only allow but encourage him to learn as much as he could about whatever he was interested in. So when he was six or seven, he started researching rain forests. Before long he could name every genus and species under the canopy. Once he learned to identify the animals, he started developing his talents by drawing them. He developed those talents so well that he ended up taking first place in the art competition at the Utah State Fair. His interest shifted over the years to other hobbies like skateboarding, the *Lord of the Rings*, medieval-style sword fighting, writing, cartooning, playing the piano, composing music, and BYU football, and his thirst for knowledge evolved into a lifelong love of learning.

When he and Clarissa were teenagers, we enrolled them in Kimber Academy, a faith-based private school. They loved it there, and both of them flourished.

Clarissa finished and was accepted at BYU. Ian wanted to follow in her footsteps. Kimber's stated goal was to help boys graduate by fifteen so that after two years of independent study courses and two years of ordinary college classes, the young men could graduate with a bachelor's degree before leaving to serve a mission. Ian was well on his way.

His life was full of many other good things as well. Active in Scouting, he lacked only his final project to become the family's first Eagle Scout. He grew to be a very talented artist. Although he was only fifteen, a local newspaper wanted to use and perhaps even syndicate his cartoons. He had a passion for football and dreamed of playing tight end, first for Lone Peak High School and then for BYU.

But above all, Ian loved music, and he had a gift! He used to love watching me sit at a digital piano and write songs. One day he asked me to teach him, so I showed him a few basic things on the piano and taught him a few simple chord progressions. The next thing I knew, he was practicing for hours every day. Over time he began writing very complex, layered, and fully orchestrated pieces of music. By the time he was fifteen, he had composed some of the most beautiful songs I had ever heard. I often said his music was not of this world. With him, music was more than an obsession; it was his calling.

Ian and I had been looking forward to my having a few rare days off work over Christmas so we could spend a lot of time together, recording the dozens of songs he had composed. Since he didn't really read music very well, he didn't know how to annotate it, so the only way to capture his creations was to record them on our digital keyboard then transfer them to my computer. I couldn't bear the thought of ever losing them, so we planned to record all of them on Christmas Eve day. After a good night's rest, we planned to get an early start. But Ian's rest ended up being an eternal one, and his music was lost.

Ian literally died with his music still inside him.

Not having those beautiful compositions recorded is one of the lingering regrets that continues to haunt me.

Losing Ian was one of the very hardest things about the accident. A wonderful bond between us was born as soon as he was. I was so grateful for a son that lived, to begin with. On top of that, he loved the same things I loved, and that drew us even closer. Ian became one of my very best friends. His life was a true gift.

I was proud of Ian for so many reasons. He was tall, strong, spiritual, kind, devoted, fun, well liked, and at times hilarious. We all seemed to act like goofballs when Ian was around.

Ian, Gary, Caleb, and Julianna, clowning around at home.

Let me give you a simple example of the kind of crazy things Ian did all the time. It was late Halloween afternoon less than two months before the accident. The phone rang in my office, where I had spent the whole day dressed as King Midas. Ian *loved* holidays, and Halloween was probably his third favorite behind Christmas, when he *really* shined, and Easter, when he was always king of the family Easter egg hunt, much to the dismay of his younger siblings. On this particular afternoon, he sounded extremely stressed. I could sense that he was anxious, so I asked, "Hey, bud. What's the matter?"

He told me he had outgrown all of the costumes we had and he was desperate for an idea. He was struggling to think of something whacky enough to surprise everyone at the church Halloween party. I was swamped at work and didn't feel like I had very much time to brainstorm

## He Can Heal

with him, but I wanted to help. I thought for a minute then said, "Well, you've got a good imagination. Why don't you just go out and take a quick look around the garage to see what you can find?"

I figured that with his goofy sense of humor and all the junk we had sitting in our garage he was sure to think of *something*.

Greg Kofford, the bishop of our ward, attended the party that night. This is how he later described what he saw when Ian showed up at the church:

> Several months ago, our youth were planning a party for Halloween in which we were all to arrive here at the church in costume. As I walked down the hallway that night, I looked ahead of me and I saw this *mass* kind of waddling toward me. As it got closer, I realized that it was Ian. He was dressed as a *mattress*! He had cut a hole in a twin-sized mattress just big enough for his face to go through; two arm holes on the side; and his legs poking through the bottom. Somehow he had managed to get himself inside it! I went up to him and asked, "How on earth did you get here?"
>
> He said, "I waddled down the street."
>
> It had taken him forty-five minutes to walk the block and a half from his house!
>
> "You'd be amazed at the faces that people made as they drove by, looking at me walking down the road," he said with a huge laugh![37]

The bishop wondered what would happen if Ian fell over backward. He didn't have to wonder for long. It turned out that, for many of the youth, the best part of the party that night was playing "flip the mattress." The kids all took turns tipping Ian over, just so they could watch him struggle, like a turtle on its back, trying to get back up.

As the bishop greeted Ian just before his weekly priests quorum meeting a few days later, he asked him, "How did you ever think of being a *mattress*?"

Ian tilted his head and smiled with that coy, infectious smile that he always had. "Well, I've always been a softie at heart!"

He certainly had.

But the most significant word that comes to mind when I think about Ian is the word *chosen*.

When Ian was very young, some of his friends introduced him to some things we had worked hard to shelter him from at home. He was somewhat ill-prepared for this, and he made a few mistakes. They weren't monumental ones, but they were significant enough that he found himself at a crossroad, with some difficult choices to make. Thankfully, he had a good heart and cared more about *being* good than *looking* good. He felt prompted to come to me and tell me what had happened. That led to some very sacred heart-to-heart talks. We counseled together, we prayed together, we cried together. Ultimately, Ian chose to courageously follow all the steps of repentance and committed to be strictly obedient.

He wanted to make things right.

From that moment on, I felt at peace about him. I felt certain that no matter what happened to him, for as long as he lived, Ian would always be just fine. You see, he had already made up his mind how he would handle difficult choices; he had already *chosen.* He had gotten to the point that he really seemed to understand the gospel of Jesus Christ, and he wanted with all his heart to do what was right. There was no need to threaten him with punishment or bribe him with rewards; he wanted to be good. From that point on, I felt that if he ever made a mistake, he would be willing to pay the price and do whatever it took to set things right with the Lord. The fact that he had made that choice was what made *him* choice.

Ian loved Christmas more than anyone I know. Almost every day from the time Santa made his annual appearance at the tail end of the Macy's parade, Ian would wear a Santa hat everywhere he went. He loved it all: hanging the lights, decorating the house, setting up our family's several nativity sets, the music, the stories—everything. For someone who loved Christmas—and Christ—so much, I can think of no greater gift on that most special of all days than the one he got—to stand in the Savior's presence.

Oh, how I loved Ian!

As I lifted his lifeless body back onto his seat, I thought back fondly to the moment when we had raced into the store. I ran through the whole scene in my mind. My heart ached as I recalled the incredible celebration we'd had. As I pondered how long it might be before I could ever hold my son again and as grief began to overcome me, the Lord blessed me with another of His many tender mercies. My mind caught hold of the memory of us hugging and jumping around in circles. I remembered the cherished moment right before we parted. We had never been happier.

Just before he turned to leave, Ian had enthusiastically grabbed me by the shoulders, turned me around to look me squarely in the eyes, flashed his bright smile, and said, "I love you, Dad!"

I have gratefully relived that treasured moment with him thousands of times. I have also been haunted almost as often by the memory of him dying in my arms. In one quiet moment of reflection months after the accident, I thought, "What the Lord required of me was a hard thing! How could I be asked to offer up my beloved son?"

How indeed could *anyone*? But who was *I* to complain? Had God asked anything less of Father Abraham? Had He required anything less of *Himself*?

Joseph Smith once told the Twelve, "You will have all kinds of trials to pass through. And it is quite as necessary for you to be tried as it was for Abraham . . . God will feel after you, and He will take hold of you and wrench your very heart strings, and if you cannot stand it you will not be fit for an inheritance in the Celestial Kingdom of God."[38]

How could I—or anyone—ever hope to inherit the same glory that great men and women of the past had inherited without being willing to endure the same kind of trials they had? But how and where could a person ever find the courage to do that?

In my case, I found it in my son. When difficult choices were placed before him, they seemed simple because he had decided in advance. I wanted to be a little more like Ian.

In the end, because he was a man who *had* chosen, he became a man who *was* chosen.

# 12

## Angels, Seen and Unseen, Came to Help

CALEB, WHO HAD BEEN SITTING beside me in the backseat of the car when we were hit, was both groggy from sleeping and dazed from the impact. As he began to be more alert, he grew more and more agitated. Although he was frightened, he was even more *confused*. He seemed to have no idea what had happened. He kept looking around, but nothing seemed to be registering in his mind.

There was so much happening on every side of him that his senses seemed to be on overload. It was more than he could handle. Clarissa, who was still trapped right beside him, was screaming and writhing in pain. It was so unsettling that with frightened tears he shouted frantically, "Stop screaming! You're *scaring* me!"

Even more frightening than her shrieks were the awful sights on every side of him. But, by the grace of God, he would somehow never remember seeing them. Right in front of him, his mother lay slumped over in the front seat, dead. In his lap lay the head of his best friend and older brother, Ian. As I saw him, surrounded by all the horrific carnage, I knew I had to get him out of there. I immediately stepped out of the car then leaned back in, reaching over to where he sat, and lifted my twelve-year-old son to pull him toward me. Before I lifted him out completely, I wanted to reassure him. I sat him on the edge of the seat for a moment. He was shivering from the cold and trembling with fear. Mustering all of the courage I could and trying not to cry, I held his face in my hands and tried to help him understand. "Hey, bud, we've been in a really bad accident. I don't think Mom and Ian are going to make it."

He just listened and never said a thing. I continued, "I love you, buddy. Everything's going to be okay."

I then lifted him out and sat him gently on the curb. The moment I set him down, paramedics swarmed him and immediately removed his coat and shirt to examine him. It was freezing cold, and he was scared and confused. I felt so sorry for him.

As I hovered over them, watching, I happened to look up and see two people standing on a little snow-covered knoll just beyond the front of the car. The fact that they hadn't been ushered away led me to assume they must either be witnesses who had seen the whole thing or people who had stopped to help. For some reason, my eyes were drawn to the one on the left, a woman, who stood with her hands cupped over her mouth in horror. From the look of compassion in her eyes, it seemed she wanted to help, but the poor woman was barely able to cope with the unbearable scene herself. She simply stood there, frightened and cold, seemingly not knowing what to do. What *could* a person do in a situation like that? How hard it must have been to come upon such a scene!

It must have surprised her when I suddenly and purposefully walked over to speak to her. Although I had absolutely no idea who she was, in *my* mind she might just as well have been an angel sent to help us. I looked in her eyes and pleaded with her, "Excuse me. My son is cold and scared . . . and he just lost his mom and his brother."

The pain seemed to grow more unbearable each time I thought about or said those words. Still I continued, "Do you think, maybe, you could just go sit by him and comfort him?"

Fighting back tears and without even moving her hands from her face, she nodded quickly a few times then nervously shuffled over to the curb. With no thought at all for herself and with all the tenderness of a loving mother, she sat down beside him, put her arm around his shoulder, and gently started to rub his back. Her soothing voice and reassuring touch would be among the few things he would remember from the whole ordeal. This kind and thoughtful stranger, whoever she was, strengthened us at a time when we needed it the very most.

To this day, I do not know who she was. If it was you, *thank you*! You made more of a difference than you will ever know!

I wouldn't see Caleb again for nine or ten hours. While I was being coaxed away from the car to the back of an ambulance—presumably to protect me from even more trauma—a team of paramedics was ushering Caleb into a separate ambulance to rush him away to Primary Children's Hospital in Salt Lake City. He remembered as little about the ambulance ride as he did about the accident. What he *did* recall was the kindness of the people who were with him. They went out of their way to help him and make him comfortable. Although they knew that his mother and brother were already gone, they had to somehow try to keep his spirits up. How hard that must have been for them!

When I asked what recollections he had, Caleb said, "I just remember a kind of a lighthearted feeling."

What an astonishing comment, and what a tribute to all of the men and women who helped him. The serenity and peace Caleb felt would always be proof to me that angels, seen and unseen, came to help.

# 13
## Comfort and Joy

CALEB, LIKE IAN, HAD COME to us in the wake of tremendous adversity. On September 21, 1992, when Clarissa was almost five and Ian nearly two, Cheryl gave birth to a baby girl, who we named Brianna Corrinne, after her older sister who had died. She was a beautiful, happy, healthy girl who filled our home with joy and laughter. Clarissa and Ian were thrilled to have a baby sister, and we were even *more* excited to have finally been able to have two healthy babies in a row! Or so we thought.

One Sunday, when Bri was about six months old, we were sitting in sacrament meeting. Our little girl seemed like she was tired and not feeling well. Partway through the hour-long meeting, she threw up. Since she looked lethargic and unhappy, we decided to get her checked. Being a Sunday, the doctor's office was closed, so we drove her to the emergency room at Primary Children's Hospital. We were grateful that *this* time we were there for something simple like the stomach flu.

A nurse escorted us back to a room where our daughter could be examined. She commented on what a beautiful baby Brianna was as she went through her normal routine of taking her temperature, checking her pulse, and jotting down her length, weight, and the circumference of her head. As she finished the last measurement, she suddenly picked up the forms we had filled out, stared at them for a second, then excused herself, saying she was finished and was going to get the doctor.

In the meantime, Cheryl tried to cheer up Brianna by blowing tummy zerberts on her bare belly, but instead of squealing and giggling with her typical contagious laughter, Bri barely even smiled. We knew she was feeling awful.

The nurse returned a few moments later with the doctor. He looked at Bri only briefly, shined a light in her eyes, then came over to us, sat down, and with a very serious expression said, "Given your family's history, we'd like to do a CT scan. Your daughter's head seems unusually large for her age, and we want to make sure there isn't something more serious going on."

For twenty minutes we sat and worried. We waited uneasily and prayed nearly the entire time. When the doctor returned, he showed us the scan and explained what we were seeing. He didn't need to. It was all too familiar.

"I'm afraid your daughter has a brain tumor."

Cheryl let out a desperate cry of shock and horror. It was more than just knowing that Bri had a tumor: it was the understanding of everything that went with it. Worse than the *dia*gnosis was the *pro*gnosis, and worse than the news of a tumor was the memory of the whole painful, drawn-out, torturous process we had gone through before with Jordan.

Thus began another ordeal—one that the Lord would use to change our hearts, to bring us to Christ, and to mold us into something more.

A few days later, Brianna would go through a nine-hour brain surgery. Thankfully, her outcome was far better than Jordan's had been. The surgeon was able to remove 95 percent of the tumor.

Over the next five months, our daughter would endure a half dozen more surgeries and numerous rounds of painful and nauseating chemotherapy until only two tiny specs of her once-massive tumor remained. I remember how excited we grew for her next MRI. The day we had prayed for finally arrived when we expected to hear the sweet words we had waited so long to hear: the cancer is in remission.

The doctor called us in to show us the scan. "Here's the image from last time," he began. "I'm sure you remember that these two tiny white specs were all that was left of the tumor."

We stood and looked closely at the scan, remembering the excitement we had felt then, when we saw the dramatic progress she'd made from the scan before that.

"Yeah, yeah," we said, eagerly waiting to see the latest results.

"This is the new scan," the doctor announced.

We bent forward and looked with eager anticipation, hoping to see a dramatic change. And there was one. Sure enough, there were no longer two little white specs on the scan—there were two *huge ones*! Brianna's tumor had grown resistant to the chemo.

"We've given it everything we have. At this point, there is nothing we can do. We'll try to give her as much time as we can," he said.

## He Can Heal

Perhaps we might have handled that news better if we hadn't gotten our hopes up so high. Our expectation of amazingly *good* news made the surprisingly *bad* news that much harder to hear. We were devastated because we had truly come to expect a miracle. From the marvelous surgery that removed most of the tumor to the amazing positive results of each successful round of chemotherapy, the evidence that she would be healed seemed to grow, and so did our faith. We felt so sure that things were going to be different this time. We had so much more faith than we ever had before, and hundreds of people, including many who didn't belong to our church, were praying with us. Nevertheless, it eventually became evident that no amount of prayers would change the fact that the sweet child we referred to as "our living miracle" was going to die. Our new prayer was that our faith and hope would not die with her.

To make it all even harder, Cheryl was six months' pregnant. Suddenly her joy and gratitude for the child she carried turned to dread at the thought that we might be called to go through all of this yet *again*.

Over the next three months, we watched in agony as our beloved little girl suffered in a thousand cruel and unimaginable ways. Every day she would get worse and things would appear to be so bad that we thought there was absolutely no way she could possibly lose anything else and still survive. And yet she did.

It began with her eyes—her beautiful, sparkling eyes. First one eyelid wouldn't close, then the other. Soon her eyes began to wander and move independent of one another. One by one her fingers stopped working, then her hands. Day after day we watched her body break down. Still, we continued to pray for a miracle. We never stopped believing! As long as she was with us, we knew God had the power to make her whole. Surely He had heard the prayers of so many hundreds of His righteous children.

After three months she started having problems with her organs. Eventually, she began "posturing," or growing stiff as a board and arching her back. A nurse who came to our house explained that what was happening was one of the final stages she had been trained to look for when providing hospice care. She said it was likely Bri would pass away by the following morning. We tried to prepare ourselves, and we spent every minute we possibly could with her. Although she continued posturing, she lived for another *three full weeks*, and every single day she got worse.

As the tumor continued to strangle her brain stem, she lost her ability to control her body temperature. One minute a thermometer would barely register and she would have the icy-cold touch of death; twenty minutes later we could put that same thermometer under her arm and watch it immediately shoot up as high as it would go. Her heartbeat would race for hours on end with a sound that resembled a person sequentially drumming all eight of their fingers on a table as fast as they could. Then, suddenly, it would just stop, and for thirty, sometimes forty seconds, we would wait to see if another heartbeat would ever come.

Our prayers seemed to have little effect on her suffering, but her suffering had a tremendous effect on our prayers. It wasn't just that they became more humble and resigned; they started to be more like they always should have been—for *her* instead of *us*. It was not until we were willing to surrender our will to the Lord that He was finally able to work His greatest wonder.

We had prayed without ceasing for a miraculous healing, and indeed we were about to see one! We prayed for a mighty change, and there was one. We prayed that the mercy of God would allow someone we loved to be saved, and it did. And every one of the miracles we saw was even greater than the ones we had expected!

Which is a greater miracle: for the Lord to heal a little baby girl with cancer or to allow that precious child to die and then heal the aching heart of her grieving mother? For months we had been praying for a mighty change in Brianna, while God's purpose all along was to cause a mighty change to be wrought in *us*. We prayed that the Lord would have mercy and that our daughter's life would be saved, without recognizing until the end that because of His mercy, we *all* would be saved. As we learned to love in a more Christlike way, we came to see hundreds of miracles all around us, including many that had been wrought in our own hearts. As we came to know God better and as we became more and more immersed in His love, our perspective became an eternal one and our sorrow began to become sweet.

Brianna finally passed away in our arms. Caleb was born three weeks later on January 2, 1994. It was difficult and strange at first to adjust to a new baby. At fourteen months old, Brianna was long and solid, heavy and pale, and the little bit of hair she had left on her head was blonde. Caleb, on the other hand—who was not only a newborn but a "preemie" (born three weeks early)—was tiny, fragile, and seemingly weightless; he had a ruddy red complexion and a full bushy head of dark brown hair. He looked like a little Eskimo baby. When a nurse first handed him to his mother, Cheryl looked down at him, careworn and seemingly unattached. She stared, wondering, "Who is this? This isn't my baby. This isn't my Bri."

It only took a few hours for them to begin to bond and for the magic of Caleb's peace-giving spirit to touch Cheryl and make her cherish him. The beautiful, tender love between them would never stop growing.

When I gave Caleb a name and a blessing in church a few weeks later, I promised him that he would be a "joy and a comfort to [his] mother all the days of her life." He truly was: when he was born, he filled her empty arms; as he grew, he healed her aching heart; and as he obeyed, he filled her with unspeakable joy and boundless love.

Since Caleb was homeschooled almost all of his life, his mom would become his favorite teacher, and his siblings would become his very best friends. That made losing them all the more difficult. Like Ian, Caleb was gifted at music, art, and acting. I taught him the same little bit about writing music that I had taught Ian, and he did exactly the same thing his brother had—he practiced nonstop until he became proficient. I also taught him to draw, and by the time he was eleven, he was producing the kind of professional-quality portraits I wasn't able to do until I was in college.

When he was eight, Caleb went to watch one of Clarissa's auditions at the Children's Theatre and was so intrigued that he begged for a chance to try out. He was bashful, reserved, and only eight at the time. Although I really didn't think he had a chance at getting a part, I allowed him to try. Not only did he make it into the cast, he ended up playing the main character in *The Best Christmas Pageant Ever* and stole the show! He later did the same in *The Great Brain*, *Where the Wild Things Are*, *Young Tommy Edison*, *Midas and the Golden Touch*, and over *thirty* other productions. Jon Adams, a director from Hale Centre Theatre in West Valley City who saw Caleb perform at the Children's Theatre as a ten-year-old, asked him to audition for *Camelot*. He got the part of Thomas of Warwick and later did many other plays at Hale Centre Theatre as well, playing Chip in *Beauty and the Beast*, plus key roles in *The Nerd*, *Big*, *A Christmas Carol*, *Miracle Worker*, and more. That led to roles in movies. He played young King Alfred in the movie *The Saxon Chronicles* and appeared with Clarissa, Ian, Julianna, and me in some of the Liken the Scriptures movies, including *Samuel the Lamanite*, in which he played a precocious Nephite child named Jarom.

The German poet Johann von Goethe once said, "Talents are best nurtured in solitude; character is best formed in the stormy billows of the world."[39]

When the accident robbed him of his mother, brother, and sister, it provided a solitude that truly allowed Caleb's talents to flourish. The accident also proved to be yet another of the stormy billows that would forge his character into something as inspiring and beautiful as his art and music.

Now, whenever I sing the Christmas song, "God Rest Ye Merry Gentlemen," I often think of my son. "From God our Heavenly Father a blessed Angel came."[40] That's the way I have always felt about Caleb.

Over the years since the accident, whenever I struggle I take a moment to look into his sparkling eyes, and the spirit of peace and acceptance that he radiates always soothes my soul. From that fateful Christmas Eve, he has filled *my* empty arms, just as he had once filled his mother's. In every way he has fulfilled the promise made to him as a baby by bringing us tidings of comfort and joy.

# 14

## A Small Ray of Hope

SHORTLY AFTER WE WERE HIT, while I was still waiting for the police and paramedics to arrive, I realized I couldn't find Julianna anywhere. I frantically concluded that she must have been thrown from the car. As soon as that thought entered my mind, I ran out into the street to look for her. Forgetting my own pain in a rush of adrenaline, I scoured the road between the intersection and the spot where we had come to a stop, desperately looking for any sign of her. Anxiously, almost hysterically, I ran all around wondering, *Where's Julie? My girl! My poor little girl!*

Julie had been another of our miracles. By the time Caleb was four and a half, it had become sadly evident that we were done having children. We each wanted more, but they just didn't come. Cheryl grew more and more uneasy. I tried to console myself. Having had seven, we had already surpassed our own expectations. Sadly, only three of those seven remained with us. But, oh, how we loved those three!

Cheryl spoke often of a feeling that we weren't done having children, but she was already thirty-nine. It seemed our time was running out. The risk of birth defects grew much higher after age forty, and every one of our pregnancies had already been considered high risk. Although Cheryl remained undeterred, we tried and prayed in vain. Whenever we would find out she wasn't pregnant, she would grieve as if she had lost another child. It was as if we had a funeral every single month for years.

Eventually her longings grew so great that we decided it was time for a blessing. One Sunday evening we invited our home teacher over. Ever consistent and faithful and always doing more than was asked, Dan Diddle was a great man, a great home teacher, and a great friend.

We pulled out a chair and had Cheryl sit down. The entire family gathered around to unite their faith. After an earnest prayer, Dan anointed

Cheryl with consecrated oil, and I sealed the anointing. As I did, the Spirit prompted me in no uncertain terms that we were not finished having children. I was surprised to hear myself tell Cheryl that her womb would be opened and she would yet bear children—not *a child*, mind you, but *children*. The very next month, Cheryl announced she was pregnant. Nine months later, in June of 1999, Cheryl gave birth to a sweet, healthy baby girl. We named her Julianna Janae.

"Juju beans" was our little princess. She grew to be a beautiful little girl with blonde curls and brown eyes. Clarissa taught her all about how to get spoiled by me. She definitely mastered it.

Julie was always the center of attention. She loved to sing, dance, and act at the Salt Lake Children's Theatre. She even acted with Clarissa and me in a Liken movie called *Alma and Abinadi*. At seven she joined a performing group, Up with Kids, that was preparing a *High School Musical* performance for just after Christmas.

Two years after Julie was born, we had another child, just as Cheryl was promised. Though Cheryl's hair was graying and her loving hands began to wrinkle, she decided to descend into the valley of the shadow of death one more time to bring a child into the world. She mustered all her courage, determined to bear one more.

This pregnancy was pretty much like the rest. She wasn't bothered by morning sickness or swollen legs. Physically she did great, gaining a very modest amount of weight, although she still condemned herself for not weighing the same as she did when we first got married. But every pound was a badge of honor and a symbol of sacrifice. To me, she was as beautiful as the day we met.

Every now and then, when we were in the temple, I would look across the room and marvel at how she had the radiance and beauty of a temple matron. She was ageless. Her eyes sparkled with love, and her countenance was full of light. She was beautiful because she was good. You cannot feign goodness, nor can you hide it.

Her pregnancy passed by slowly with the same worries and stresses as before: appointments with the obstetrician, who reminded us of all the risks of having a child after forty; ultrasounds with perinatologists to be sure we wouldn't have to face another tumor; and so on.

Thankfully, everything progressed as it should, and the blessed day finally arrived. Uncertain if she had the emotional strength for a long labor, Cheryl decided to deliver our last child via Caesarean. She was finally growing weary.

Charles Dickens's famous character Nicholas Nickleby eventually married a young woman, who, like Cheryl, had dedicated herself to selflessly serving one she loved. Acknowledging both her strength in adversity and the toll that it had taken on her, Nicholas observes, "Weakness is tiring, but strength is exhausting."[41]

Cheryl was exhausted. The toll had grown too steep and the risks too many and too great to go any further. All she had ever wanted was to be a mother, so the thought of surrendering the ability to bear children was dreadful and distressing; nevertheless, she reluctantly conceded that this would be her last child.

On June 4, 2001, Brayden Garrett was born. Holding our adorable newborn son and knowing that she had sprinted through the finish line, Cheryl was at peace. That peace was short-lived, as Brayden, too, would be. His unexpected difficulty breathing prompted doctors to send him to the newborn ICU at another hospital. As I had done years before with Jordan, I escorted him to the helipad to be transported by Life Flight helicopter. Cheryl, restricted once again to a wheelchair as she recovered, would travel from one hospital to another to visit a son in an intensive care unit. The parallels with the past were uncanny.

For three weeks doctors supplemented Brayden's oxygen and tried to help as he struggled with his suck-and-swallow reflex. When he ate, it was difficult for him to breathe. The ability to simultaneously breathe and swallow is a basic instinct people are normally born with—one that they don't need to think about, like their heartbeat, breathing, and blinking—things that are all controlled . . . in the *brain stem*. A doctor, reviewing the family history, had an "aha" moment and ordered an MRI. Brayden, just three weeks old, was diagnosed with the same rare tumor that had taken Jordan and Brianna. It had only been seen fifty-four times in all of recorded medical history and never more than once in the same family, not amongst siblings, cousins, or even *generations*. Never! Yet this was our *third*? After the first one, we were told there was only a 1 in 500,000,000 chance it would ever happen again, but it did happen again—twice.

Our visits to the children's hospital were emotional. We became reacquainted with doctors and nurses who had gone through all this with us before. Day after day we went through the all-too-familiar routine of giving neupogen shots, changing broviac dressings, and watching for infections. There was also lots of joy, family love, and the special growth and tenderness of heart that came from caring for a child with special needs. Once again our hearts and home were sanctified as we were asked once more to let a child go. He fought a good fight. In fact, we all did. But Brayden finally passed away in February of 2002.

As Ian had once restored our joy when we lost three babies in a row, and Caleb had comforted us when Bri died, Julianna's sweet smile soothed our soul when Brayden passed away. We thought she would always be there for us.

But where was Julie now? I couldn't find her anywhere! I was terrified about where she might be, completely overwhelmed by everyone else's condition, and worried about the condition of the car. Fearing that it could possibly burst into flames or explode, I became even more hyped on adrenaline and abruptly switched into action mode.

*I've got to get everyone out of here!* I thought. I tugged frantically on Cheryl's door, but it wouldn't budge. It didn't occur to me at the time, but looking back, I realize it was probably just locked. I raced around to Ian and Clarissa's side. Looking at the back of the car as I passed behind it, it didn't even seem like we'd been hit very badly, but as I continued around to the side that was hit, I saw something I wasn't prepared to see. The accident had been so violent it had twisted the car into a crescent shape.

I realized there was no way I could possibly extricate either of my older children, so I raced back to the other side, climbed into the back, and reached over my wife's backrest to try to lift her back up against her seat.

As I knelt there looking down at my precious wife, about to try to gently raise her by the shoulders, it occurred to me that with the way she was slumped over, it was possible that Julianna might actually be right *there*, underneath her. Slowly, I reached forward and slid my hand underneath her to see if I could find anything. Suddenly my fingertips pressed against skin. They had landed on the side of Julianna's neck, right on her jugular vein. Although it seemed unusually heavy, her pulse was strong. After all my frantic searching, I had found Julianna.

My heart leapt for joy at finding that my sweet little daughter was still alive, and I thanked the Lord for sending a small ray of hope.

# 15
## The Heart of a Hero

As soon as the paramedics arrived and Caleb was settled on the curb, I raced over and tried to get the attention of one of the rescue workers. Approaching the nearest EMT, I cried out, "My daughter is trapped. Please save her!"

I knew he would have to hurry if Julianna was going to have any chance of making it.

With an intense look of urgency, determination, and compassion, the paramedic immediately rushed to look for her. I learned later how my plea had echoed in his ears. For more than four hours, he and others desperately gave their all to save her. I will always think of Joseph Treadwell, the man who pulled Julianna from the wreckage, as a true hero.

In May of 2007, Joseph was named EMT of the Year for his courageous and tireless efforts that night. Chris Frazier, reporter for the *Salt Lake Tribune*, wrote a powerful and moving article about Joseph's efforts and his acceptance speech at the award ceremony. I quote below from that article and a transcript of Mr. Treadwell's speech:

> Christmas Eve 2006 is a day Joseph Treadwell finds difficult to talk about . . . It was on that day . . . in the early morning hours when children in homes across the country were anticipating the arrival of Santa Claus that the Murray City Fire Department captain and emergency medical technician was rushing to the scene of a two-car crash. He knew by the tone of the dispatcher's voice that the accident was critical.
>
> Treadwell was among the second crew of emergency service responders to arrive only minutes after [the accident]. The story few heard about from that day was Treadwell's effort to save Julianna's life . . .

Treadwell says he was standing near the Ceran's car during the rescue when he was told that there was a little girl pinned beneath her mother in the front seat . . .

"Initial crews had believed that no one in the front seat had survived, but when I heard her father's words, I knew I had to find a way to get to her without waiting for the extrication," he said. "When I finally reached her and pulled her into my arms, I knew we had to do everything we could to save her."

Treadwell gave Julianna rescue breaths as he carried her from the car to the waiting ambulance. He continued the resuscitation efforts inside the ambulance until Life Flight arrived and transported the girl to Primary Children's Medical Center.

[The memory] is something he can't help but carry with him, he said, not only because of a senseless tragedy that happened on Christmas Eve to a family, but also because of Julianna's similarity with his own daughter.

"It's difficult to deny how you feel when the patient in front of you is the same age, has the same flowing hair, has the same feeling as the daughter you hugged earlier in the day . . . It's always there. You try to smile and hide what you feel, but the ache is there and will be for a while."

In fact, Treadwell's acceptance speech paints an even clearer picture of his feelings that night:[42]

> I would like to accept this award for all of those who have spent most of their lives serving our cities and towns in this world we know as EMS. It is both privilege and duty that carries us onward. And although I am the one recognized today, my peers with tenure in this profession know very well the price and the reward of our service.
>
> They have heard the tones go off late at night, and known by the slightest change in a dispatcher's voice they've heard a hundred times before, that this call is different. They know the feel of arriving on a scene of twisted metal and leaking anti-freeze. Quickly assessing the carnage amongst the deafening silence of the ones who do not cry out for help. They know the helplessness in waiting

for the extrication to release this deadly metal's grip so you can do what you've trained day after day for. They have experienced the emotional evisceration that erupts when you discover the lifeless patient in your arms is only seven years old and feels just like the daughter you hugged when you left for work that day. And perhaps they too have pleaded with God between rescue breaths, the one prayer they waited their whole career to use, "Lord, please let me heal like Jesus did . . . Please, Lord, it's Christmas Eve . . . just let me heal like Jesus did."

And then to gather your scattered gear amongst the stained white sheets and ask yourself why . . . until someone mentions something about a drunk driver. And as those words scream in your head, you never even hear the roar of the helicopter taking off.

To know what it's like to go home the next morning with aching hollowness inside, yet you smile and try to hide your family from the pain of what you've seen. But each time your seven-year-old daughter hugs you that day, or sings her Christmas song, you feel the wind suck out of your body as you're reminded that there is a father (praying) at that very same moment . . . begging to feel those little arms around his neck just one more time.

And then another day comes, the uniform goes on, the ache is still there and will be for a while; it all comes with the career we've chosen. But ironically you can't ever imagine giving that duty to anyone else; to leave this community would be far more painful.[43]

When I read this article six months after the accident and reflected on that moment and the expression on the face of that paramedic, I marveled at how it actually seemed that his heartache rivaled my own. May God bless Joseph Treadwell and all the brave and selfless men and women like him who did—and continue to do—so much to try to save innocent lives. Every one of them truly has the heart of a hero.

# 16

## The Heartache and the Hopelessness

THERE WAS CHAOS AND COMMOTION all around as policemen, firemen, and paramedics all worked frantically to do their respective jobs.

After turning to answer some initial questions from a police officer, I looked back toward the car and caught a glimpse of Clarissa in the backseat. Our eyes met. She looked right at me, yet she didn't seem to recognize me. She had a wild look of panic on her face and was totally glassy-eyed, obviously in shock.

As soon as rescue workers had rushed over to look for Julianna and pull her from the wreckage, one of the police officers walked up to me and started asking all sorts of questions. It was difficult for him to keep my attention. I had no desire to stand still and talk. I was pumped on adrenaline, and my only thought was to help my family. I wanted to be cooperative; nevertheless, I continued to try to push my way past the police to get back to the car. The officer tried to hold me back, but I insisted, "I have to get my family out!"

"Don't worry, son," the officer said, calmly yet firmly, gently leading me in the other direction. "There are a lot of professionals working on that right now. Your family's in good hands," he added as he kindly but insistently led me to the back of an ambulance. "You must be freezing. Let's get you warmed up."

It wasn't until much later that I eventually caught on that his main motivation for doing so wasn't his concern for my physical comfort but for how I might fare *emotionally*. He was trying to keep me away from my car so I wouldn't be marred by the images of the bodies of my loved ones being removed. Experience had taught him that getting people out could be both ugly and difficult.

By the time our interview was done and we finally came outside, the doors had been removed from the passenger side of the car and, along with them, Cheryl, Clarissa, Ian, and Julianna. I saw Clarissa's ambulance as it raced off to University of Utah Medical Center. A second ambulance sped off just behind it, hurrying Caleb to Primary Children's Hospital. By the curb, emergency workers toiled feverishly in the back of yet another ambulance to stabilize Julianna for transport by helicopter.

In retrospect, I am so grateful to both the Lord and that kind officer for protecting me that night and keeping me from seeing most of the countless traumatic sights that might have otherwise been forever seared into my memory. I can't imagine how difficult and damaging it would have been to have seen more than I did.

Today, I feel blessed to remember the accident so vividly because I was sheltered from the most graphic images that would have been too painful to cope with and impossible to forget. What I *saw* was unbearable, but what I didn't see was worse.

As I walked toward the car, I noticed a huge double body bag. By then, there was nothing more that could be done for its occupants so it had been zipped shut to hide the ghastly carnage. But I knew what it was and who was in it. There lay the earthly remains of my oldest son and my life's companion. Their voices were silenced, their lives were snuffed out, and it seemed as if they had been reduced to a heap of refuse that was just sitting by a curb, waiting to be picked up and hauled away. How senseless! How unnecessary! I just stood and stared, incredulous. They were *gone*.

The eyes that, for years, had looked back at me with love were shut, never to be opened again in this life. The arms that had hugged me were folded and lay lifeless over their chests. The voices that had cheered, encouraged, and praised me for so long were hushed forever. And I didn't even get to say good-bye.

For a singular, indescribably demoralizing moment, I stood behind my car. My only vehicle was totaled. All that was salvageable of our Christmas dinner and those last-minute gifts that had seemed so important lay strewn on the ground. In shock and disbelief, I glanced at the gnarled wreck that was once my car. I stared at the body bag, and I looked at the spots where the ambulances and helicopter had just been. I was depressed, disheartened, and dismayed.

At that moment, I didn't know where I was going. I would have three children in two different hospitals, and I would soon be going to one myself, but I had absolutely no idea how I was going to get home.

But that was really the least of my worries. I didn't know how I would ever be able to put my life back together, let alone the lives of my children. To add insult to injury, I recognized that I was going to be facing hundreds of thousands of dollars' worth of medical expenses, ambulance and helicopter transportation costs, and sundry other bills for coffins, headstones, and funerals. By the next morning, I would learn that my medical insurance application, which I had turned in two days before, had never been submitted because the person in charge of sending it to the home office had left early for the holidays.

My prospects for the future had never been so bleak, and I had never felt so discouraged in my life. Helplessness and despair hung over me like a dark cloud of doom. And worst of all, a few feet away lay that cursed body bag.

I was heartbroken, stunned, unprepared, and overwhelmed. Like never before, I felt an ominous sense of emptiness, anguish, and loneliness.

As I look back now, I realize how blind I was to how my life would truly change. There was no way I could have begun to conceive the pain that awaited me, nor could I have ever imagined the miracles my loving Father in Heaven had prepared to help me heal. In that moment I only knew the heartache and the hopelessness.

# 17

## He Changed My Heart

ONCE I WAS SECURELY STRAPPED on the gurney, the ambulance pulled away from the scene of the accident. As I collected my thoughts, it occurred to me that I needed to let people know what had happened. A feeling of dread came over me as I contemplated the phone calls I was about to make. What words can one use to share something so horrible? And how would I find the strength to say them?

I stared blankly at the ceiling, suddenly overcome with a sadness I had never known, and thought, *I can't do this.*

Unfortunately I had no choice, so I nervously dialed the number of my brother Erol in Northern California. Just two years older than me, he had always been one of my best friends. I thought of the scripture in Proverbs that says, "A friend loveth at all times . . . a brother is born for adversity."[44] Surely this was adversity! I needed his help so desperately, but I couldn't imagine how I could tell him what happened. My heart raced as I considered what I might say. The phone rang several times without an answer. Almost relieved, I hung up. Just as I looked at my phone to press End Call, it started to vibrate. I could see that Erol was calling me back.

The sound of my brother's voice comforted me, yet his words—and the love and concern with which he said them—brought to the surface a thousand emotions that had evidently been suppressed by coursing adrenaline.

"Gar? Are you all right?"

I struggled to think of how to respond. After a short pause, my voice began breaking as my sorrow swelled, and I forced out the only answer I could think of: "No." My voice was almost like a whimper, and he knew from my answer and the way that my voice was faltering that something was terribly wrong.

"What's happened?" he asked, his voice already aching at the thought.

You see, we'd had conversations like this too many times before: first, when Cheryl and I lost our twins . . . then Jordan . . . and Brianna . . . and Brayden. I could tell Erol was trying to be strong for me, but I could hear in his voice that he was struggling mightily to brace himself. My voice quivered. Finally, I mustered, "We've been in an accident."

There was almost a sense of *relief* in his voice as he assumed that, for once, it was something other than a death. But that feeling of relief quickly turned to an even more heart-wrenching sense of shock and horror.

"Is everyone okay?" he asked apprehensively, anticipating a positive and reassuring answer.

I gulped hard and tried to gather the strength to respond. Once again, all I could manage to get out was, "No."

As I tried to figure out how to say what I wanted so badly to *not* have to say, my mind began to catch hold of the dreadfulness of what had actually just happened. I guess it hadn't fully registered yet. "Ian didn't make it," I blurted out.

My eyes were suddenly brimming with tears, and my voice was faltering in small sobs. It was so shocking that it seemed like the news reached my ears at the very moment it reached his. Pain pierced my heart like a javelin. It was awful to consider the grim and distressing words that had just escaped my lips, and it only compounded my sorrow that I had just brought that same kind of pain to my brother. And I wasn't done. "Neither did Cheryl," I added, breaking down.

"Oh, Gar," he cried out in disbelief. "No!"

He evidently wasn't any more prepared to lose any of them than I was. The overwhelming tragedy of it all was only beginning to set in as I continued, "They're trying to save Julie right now."

"Where are you?" he asked.

"I'm in the back of an ambulance on my way to the University of Utah Medical Center."

Without a moment of hesitation, he spoke the only words of comfort he could. "I'm on my way."

What else *could* he say? What else could he *do*? I cannot even begin to imagine how difficult it must have been to receive such a call in the middle of the night and hear something so totally heartbreaking, but that did not deter him. I have no idea how he was able to manage it, but he immediately set things in motion, and within a few hours, he was there by my side.

As soon as the trauma of that call had ended, I was forced to repeat the whole awful ordeal two more times. I phoned our bishop, then Glenn Kimber, a close family friend, and asked them to notify our friends and extended family. After making those agonizing calls, I lay back in silence for a few moments, trying to recover emotionally and take it all in.

I began to pray for what was left of my family. I was so worried about Clarissa and Caleb. I had so many serious concerns about how their futures were going to be affected by the accident. Thankfully, at least I didn't have to fear for their physical lives. The same could not be said of Julianna, who was on the brink of joining the others.

Lying helpless on a stretcher in the back of an ambulance, I struggled to grasp the scope of what was happening. The adrenaline that had carried me was beginning to fade. As it did, I began to become increasingly aware of intense pain. Meanwhile, time seemed like an enigma. Everything was happening so fast, yet it all seemed to be happening in slow motion. Although many of the ramifications of what happened that night would not be apparent for quite some time, I knew one thing: my wife was gone and so was my son. I just kept muttering, "My family! My family!"

Memories of Cheryl and Ian raced through my mind. Desperately, I tried to cling to precious images, but they just kept slipping through like sand through an hourglass, appearing barely long enough for me to perceive them before vanishing. Tens of thousands of wonderful moments flooded my mind, each more wonderful and, consequently, more painful than the last. In horror, I lay and reflected on what was happening. In my anguish there were three things I simply couldn't seem to get out of my mind: the thunderous sound of the collision, Clarissa's wailing in pain, and the deafening silence I had heard when I called out to Cheryl. I couldn't stop thinking about all I had lost—or about my precious little girl who was fighting for her life.

As I thought about sweet little Julianna's battle for survival, my heart reached out to God, and I began to cry out from the depths of my soul for my daughter. I prayed, quite literally, like I had never prayed before. I had prayed for my children every morning and night from the day they were born and even before. I had pleaded with the Lord each time they were ill. I had even poured out my heart many times when one of their lives hung in the balance. Time after time, I had pleaded for the life of a child to be spared. As my yearnings began to find a familiar voice, my mind returned to those impassioned pleas when, with the greatest sincerity and effort, I had petitioned the Lord for a miraculous healing. It almost felt as if my life was flashing before my eyes, as I remembered the heart-wrenching, soul-stretching anguish of each trial and prayer.

But this time something was different. As I began to pray, I didn't struggle at all to find the right words; they just seemed to flow effortlessly—so much so that they scarcely felt as if they were my own. I silently offered a different prayer than I had ever offered before. *Father, in Heaven, I need Thee! Help me!* I began. *My daughter lies on the brink of death. My heart is breaking, Lord! Please, dear Father, strengthen my faith!*

As I said these words, I felt an incredible power come over me. In an instant my panic was turned to peace. My tensed body began to relax, and a warm soothing sense of calm enveloped me. I literally felt as if I was encircled about in the arms of His love. With an astonishing sense of relief, I sighed and took a long, deep breath. Then, with new-found strength, I continued praying. *Father, I understand. I finally understand!*

It was remarkable. Suddenly all of my life's trials made sense to me. I began to recognize how each one had helped to prepare me not only for the next, but for this very event. My heart, to my great surprise, began to be filled with immeasurable *gratitude*! In that one defining moment, I realized that something had changed inside of me. Calm assurance poured over me, and I felt something I had never felt so fully before. I was so amazed at the change taking place in me that I *smiled* and cried out within myself, *I trust Him!*

With a new heart, I concluded my prayer. As I voiced the words in my head, I was shocked at what I said: *Father, I trust Thee and I will put my trust in Thee forever! Dear Father, I surrender my will to Thine. I put my daughter's life in Thy hands. Do with her as seemeth Thee good. Thou knowest how I love her; nevertheless, I know that she was Thine before she was mine. If she truly must go home to be with Thee, Lord, so be it. But, if she must, dear God, please bless me with the faith to endure it!*

Each of the previous times one of my children had been at death's door, I had pleaded for them to *stay*. I understood that "Thy will be done" was a necessary formality that had to be acknowledged at the end of my prayers, but I always said it begrudgingly and only as an afterthought. In retrospect, it seems that I had always prayed with a sort of reluctant and frustrated resignation. I had treated my conversations with Deity almost as if I were at a sandwich shop. I would ask for what I wanted the same way I would if I were ordering a sub on Monterrey cheddar bread. I didn't like it when the deli was out of it. "Okay, fine! I'll have it on wheat."

For me saying "Thy will be done" at the end of a prayer was like settling for wheat bread. I always whined about it. It just wasn't what I really wanted.

This time something changed. I actually *wanted* His will to be done instead of my own. Somehow, it finally occurred to me that the all-wise and all-knowing God of the universe actually knew more than *I* did. I finally understood that I would be a lot better off if I would just learn to want for *myself* what *He* wanted for me. My prayer continued: *Father, I put my life in Your hands as well. I know that You know what's best for me. Please help me!*

I wasn't asking that He would change the trial and make it equal to my strength; I was asking that He would change *me* and make my strength equal to the trial.

*Father, I don't understand this!* I told Him.

I couldn't fathom why He would see fit to take even more of my family away from me. I had done this so many times before. Had I not already proven to Him that I would remain faithful? Had I not already demonstrated my faith? Did I *really* have to lose someone *again*?

As I thought back on every trial I had ever been through and what I had learned and become because of each one, I realized that in every instance, if I were taken back and given the choice to have that trial or not, *I wouldn't choose to change it.* The many times the Lord had healed me in the past bore a fervent testimony to me that He would heal me in the future, and I would be better for having been through it. I didn't know why I needed to lose them, but I knew that *He* knew.

*My heart is breaking Lord! But if this is part of Thy plan, then surely there is some purpose in this for me (and for others). Father, help me to stand! Free me from this heartache and help me to accept Thy will. Heal me of this hopelessness; fill me with Thy love; and help me to have the strength to do whatever I am called to do.*

If God knows everything (and He does), and if He loves each of us with an infinite love and desires the best for us in every instance (which He does), doesn't it make sense to *trust* Him and put our lives in His hands?

I look back on that night with tremendous gratitude.

In the accident, God changed my *life*. In the ambulance, He changed my *heart*!

# 18
## Suffering in the Emergency Room

MUCH OF MY SUFFERING IN the wee hours of that Christmas Eve morning was not so much physical as emotional. One of the first of those pains was also one of the worst. It came out of nowhere when I was filling out a registration form. I speedily filled out each line: first name, middle name, last name, address. The next line turned out to be harder than expected—"Marital status." Out of habit, without any thought, I quickly checked *married*. As my eyes continued down the page, a few inches away I stumbled across the word *widowed*. Although in my mind nothing had changed, to the world around me, I, like my life, was suddenly different.

Feeling an unfamiliar combination of sadness, embarrassment, and guilt, I scribbled out the first check mark I had made and put a mark beside *widowed*. The pain and seeming finality of it made my eyes well up with tears.

As a nurse led me back to an examination room, I noticed a warm squishy feeling in my right shoe. Looking down I noticed for the first time since I had tried to bless Ian that his blood had soaked my legs and filled my shoe. As the haunting, terrifying memory of that moment assailed my defenseless mind, my feeling of remorse and culpability began to grow worse.

I eventually learned that Ian and Cheryl had died instantly of a basal skull fracture and a severed spine. The trauma to Clarissa's leg left her in tremendous pain and unable to move from the waist down. Caleb had a cracked rib, a broken shoulder blade, and a fractured pelvis. Although I was in considerable pain, none of my injuries seemed to be particularly serious. I felt terribly guilty. Why had I not asked Ian to move? It should have been *me*, not *him*, who died. Had I just waited for him to move, we probably never would have been hit at all!

It was almost 6:30 in the morning on December 24. Although the doctor would release me in a few hours, I was still bedridden in the emergency room, being treated. The doctors had allowed my stake presidency, three of the most tenderhearted and spiritual men I have ever known, to visit me. They pushed aside the curtain and approached my bed to offer their condolences and comfort. As they were telling me what they had learned about Clarissa's and Caleb's conditions, a female doctor stepped in from the other side of the bed. Clearing her throat, she tried to get my attention.

"Mr. Ceran?"

I looked up at her, wondering who she was. "Yes," I replied.

For a long, awkward moment, she didn't say anything more. She just peered nervously at the men beside me. Sensing her uneasiness, President Swenson asked, "Do you need us to leave?"

She looked back at *me* for an answer. I shook my head side to side. "No. That's all right."

The woman, who now stood at the foot of my bed, seemed uneasy and pensive. She just stared at the floor for a moment. I would learn later that she was trying to choke back her tears. Finally, she looked up at me and said, "I'm sorry. We've been trying frantically for nearly four hours to save your little girl. They've asked me to come and let you know she didn't make it. I'm afraid she's passed away . . . just barely."

I stared straight ahead for a minute, not really looking at anything in particular, then shook my head in disbelief as the presidency gathered close around me to strengthen me with their love and faith. "Thank you," I told her. "Thank you for doing all you could."

Beginning to cry, she silently nodded, acknowledging my gratitude, then solemnly turned and walked out of the room.

"Are you okay?" President Hoffman asked.

Just as the doctor had done, I silently nodded in the affirmative. In my prayer I had told the Lord I would accept His will, no matter what it was, but losing Julianna was so very hard! I knew I had to keep my word, but it was only with His help that I would be able to.

I later learned how difficult that moment had been for everyone. The following day an article in the *Deseret News* reported that, according to Sally Dietlein, our producer from Hale Theater who was acting as a spokesperson regarding the accident, "'The nurses at Primary Children's were in tears,' said Dietlein, who visited with the survivors Sunday. 'The doctor who had to explain to the father what had happened to seven-year-old Julianna said it was the hardest thing she'd ever had to do.'"[45]

Perhaps Julie's obituary can provide some insight into what truly helped us cope: our testimony of the Lord Jesus Christ, His Resurrection, and the plan of salvation.

> Julianna Ceran, age seven, Our Little Princess, was killed in a horrific traffic accident on Christmas Eve. Joined in death by the two people on earth who could in no way bear her parting, she was taken—with her pure heart, warm smile, and sweet sense of humor—to a far better place. She longed for her eighth birthday that would allow her to be baptized, participate in *Savior of the World*, and provide her a new world of opportunities. . . . Her singing, dancing, and laughter brightened our world and have left us to abide yet another night as we wait for yet another dawn. But we know that dawn will surely come, and that one day, not far distant, we will join her at the feet of our Savior, when all our wounds are healed; and there, together, we will bathe His feet with our tears as we thank Him for His life and death and resurrection, which will allow us to be reunited.

I do not know how I could ever endure the loss of my daughter Julianna—or any of my other family members—without a sure knowledge of the Resurrection. The absence of that testimony would cause a paralyzing fear of being permanently separated from her, which is the only thing that could have worsened my almost unbearable suffering in the emergency room.

# *19*

## The Hardest Thing I'd Ever Done

Long before I would be reunited with Cheryl and our seven children who died, I would be reunited with Clarissa and Caleb. It was late in the morning on Christmas Eve day when I was released and permitted to cross the long, covered corridor that connected this hospital with Caleb's. Increasing pain made the long walk seem even longer. Like Clarissa and Caleb, my back was getting worse, and in addition to injuring both of my legs, I had an excruciating undiagnosed internal injury that would soon get so bad that I would have to be readmitted. But what made the walk worst of all was the burden I was carrying. I had just barely learned that Julianna had passed away—in the very place I was headed, in fact. Cheryl and Ian were gone as well, and to make it worse, it seemed as if they had been erased from my memory. Each time I tried to picture them alive, all I could see was that cursed, closed body bag.

I was distraught. On Christmas Eve I should have been happily helping Cheryl wrap presents for our *four* children, not dejectedly asking her in my head how to tell our *two* children that she and Ian and Julie were gone.

Clarissa and Caleb still had no idea what had happened. Friends who had visited them told me that doctors and nurses specifically asked everyone to "play dumb" and not say anything about the others. To avoid telling what they knew, several people even went so far as to nonchalantly ask how everyone else was doing. When they answered that they had no idea, it was evident that they didn't remember what they had seen.

Brother Kimber, who had been the administrator of their school, said that when he visited Caleb earlier in the day, he had asked what the boy remembered. Caleb said, "I remember Clarissa screaming a lot and a nice lady with a really soothing voice sitting next to me on the curb and rubbing my back." He paused for minute then added, "And I remember my Dad saying, 'I love you, buddy. Everything's going to be okay.'"

Strangely, of all the things I said as I lifted him out of the car, he had absolutely no recollection at all of my having said anything about Ian or his mom; the only thing he remembered was that I loved him and that everything was going to be okay. Perhaps, for him, that was enough.

As I limped gingerly down the long corridor, I thought of how difficult it must have been for his doctors and nurses to keep the sad news a secret. For hours, they were obliged to deftly dodge questions about the rest of the family. It was so strange to me that both children were awake at the scene of the accident from right after we were hit until ambulances sped them to the hospital. Much of the time, Caleb was not only alert but responding to people. Still, neither remembered what happened, and neither had any recollection at all of the horrible images that were haunting and torturing *me*. I dreaded the thought of having to share so much heartache and anguish with them. I knew this would be one of the hardest things I had ever done.

But I was still so excited to see Caleb and Clarissa! With all the death and loss, they were my only lifelines to the world I knew. Of a family of eleven, just the three of us remained.

With the gentle sweetness of Cheryl's voice, the soothing harmonies of Ian's piano compositions, and the heart-warming sound of Julie's contagious laughter all suddenly silenced, that first day in the hospital, away from my two surviving children, had been deafeningly quiet and unbearably lonely. I was surrounded with people almost constantly, but one often feels most lonely in a crowd.

Friends, family, and coworkers joined together with neighbors, people in our church congregation, and people we had performed with. All told, more than five hundred people came to visit us the first day alone. They lifted our spirits and surrounded us in Christlike love. We were so grateful! But the absence of those faces that normally filled each day with happiness left a huge gaping hole in our hearts. It wasn't just that so much of my *family* was suddenly gone; so much of my *life* was gone. I began to realize that each of them had become so much a part of my life that I literally felt as if part of *me* was missing.

Caleb's friends told me that, despite his several broken bones, Caleb seemed to be in pretty good shape—and pretty good spirits—all things considered. Physically, he looked better than expected, given what was said on the news. Doctors said they would release him as soon as he was able to climb the stairs down the hall from his room. Just over a day after the accident, he was already growing determined to attempt it, despite the pain, so he could go see Clarissa. Emotionally, the serenity and peace he radiated and the almost inexplicable twinkle in his eyes cheered and reassured everyone who came to comfort him.

It was hard for him to be alone for so long. Friends who had visited them said Caleb and Clarissa were both getting restless to see each other. They craved a taste of normalcy, like I did.

Remembering Clarissa's screaming, Caleb asked about her frequently. His nurses told him she was in a different hospital and she was okay, but little else. They also mentioned that I was going to be coming to see him, so at least for a short time that morning he had something positive to think about. That was important because he had a vivid imagination and too much time to think. He spent quite a bit of that time trying in vain to remember what happened. Thankfully, as he told me later, even with all that time, it had never occurred to him that someone could have been killed; he was only worried about who was hurt and how badly.

Several people accompanied me on the awkward and emotionally charged walk. Since Brother Kimber had already seen Caleb and knew where the room was, he led the way. He walked on one side of me, while my bishop strode on the other. As we neared the room, I was understandably excited to see Caleb, but how I was dreading what I had to do! For several minutes I was too overcome to walk in. I paced back and forth outside his door, pleading with those with me to help me know what to say. No one had any idea; they simply encouraged and reassured me that everything would be all right.

How on earth was a man supposed to share news like that with his *son*? He was only *twelve*. He was just a *boy*!

Each time I rehearsed a different way to bear the ghastly news, tears welled up in my already swollen eyes.

After a few minutes, I rallied all my courage and entered the room. My bishop stayed by the doorway at first. Brother Kimber greeted Caleb warmly and then stood by the wall. I went over and threw my arms around my son, making sure not to squeeze him too hard and hurt him. The doctor had helped him swing his legs around and sit on the left side of his bed. Seemingly in pain, he turned mostly just his eyes toward me. His head was half bowed, and he just stared straight ahead, perhaps a bit apprehensive.

He looked like a person with a stiff neck—or a bunch of broken bones, I suppose—or a person who was in some kind of trouble. I sat down next to him and took a deep breath. After a moment, I put my hand on his knee and said, "Buddy, do you have any idea what's happened?"

He didn't say a word; he just subtly shook his head back and forth a few times. How could I possibly tell him?

The moment I had been shrinking from had arrived. I swallowed hard, then I put my hands on his shoulders and looked into his eyes, as I had by the side of the car.

As I tried to get up the courage to talk, my eyes almost instantly welled up with tears, and Caleb began to sense that something was terribly wrong.

"We've been in a really bad accident," I told him.

He didn't say a word. He just tried to brace himself in something like the emotional equivalent of a karate stance.

"Clarissa's over at the U [the University of Utah Medical Center], and she really wants to see you. I just got released. I came over as soon as I could."

I paused for just a second. He looked at me with those innocent eyes and asked the obvious follow-up question: "How's everybody else?" he wondered aloud. "Where are Ian and Mom and Julie?"

I paused again, trying desperately to choke back the tears. Barely able to contain my emotions, I blurted out the dreadful words that neither of us will ever forget: "Ian didn't make it!"

I started to cry, letting out a couple of almost cough-like sobs. Even though the news had come from my own mouth, it hurt so much to hear.

"Neither did Mom," I said, crying even harder. Then, barely able to speak, my voice faltering with emotion, I added, "And neither did Julie."

Finally, overcome with grief and devastated by the harsh reality of the tragic, heartrending words I had just spoken, I broke into sobs. Bishop Nielsen put his hand on my shoulder to comfort me. It was a very sacred moment. No one said a word. Not knowing what to say, they said nothing, choosing instead to remain respectfully silent and blend into the background. They could all appreciate how hard it was for me to do this. They watched reverently and seemed to feel grateful to witness such a tender and sacred scene. I tried as hard as I could to compose myself; then, mustering what tiny measure of courage I could, I looked back at

Caleb. The moment I saw his face, I understood the real reason everyone had grown so reverent. A single tear rolled down Caleb's right cheek, then he looked at me and smiled—yes, *smiled* —and, with his eyes sparkling as they always had, he said, "That's all right, Dad; we're still a family."

What an incredible testimony! What an incredible son! It was amazing to see insight and strength like that in a twelve-year-old boy. I felt like Joseph when he found *his* twelve-year-old, Jesus, in the temple. I was given a glimpse at the man he would someday become. This was not feigned acceptance but sweet assurance. Caleb *knew* we would all be reunited and live together as a family forever. As we sat there, an incredible feeling of peace came over us, and a soft voice whispered that everything was going to be all right.

From then on Caleb was a rock. As I struggled to cope, heal, redefine myself, and ultimately move on, he filled my days with purpose, perspective, and happiness. His innocent assurance strengthened my faith, reassured me, and inspired me to keep moving forward. Caleb's strength can be seen so well in a Mormon Message that the Church created about him. You can watch the video on the Church's website at https://www.lds.org/youth/video/still-a-family?lang=eng.

Not long after telling Caleb, I repeated the whole heart-wrenching ordeal with Clarissa. We cried and hugged and found solace together in the presence of the many people who came, with Christlike love, to "mourn with those that mourn and comfort those that stand in need of comfort."[46]

I have relied on Caleb and good people like him many times to calm my troubled heart and help me feel peace in the midst of severe trials, but never more than on that day, when I had to do the hardest thing I'd ever done.

# 20
## A Gift That Keeps on Giving

WITHIN HOURS OF THE ACCIDENT, members of the media began closely following what was happening. When three members of a family lose their lives in a car crash, it's news; but when a family that has already buried five children loses two more plus their mother to a drunk driver on Christmas Eve, the story is as compelling as it is tragic.

Sometime late that same morning, after I had been readmitted, treated, and released again, I agreed to meet with several of the reporters who had been asking, through the hospital's public relations director, for an interview. Correspondents from several newspapers and television stations took turns speaking to me, as would many others over the weeks and months that followed. As we sat in the hospital lobby doing the first television interview, the reporter told me the little she had learned about the person who had been driving the truck that had run into us: "We understand from booking documents that the man who hit you was an illegal alien who was driving drunk. It is rumored that he has had other DUIs and that he was apparently driving without a license."

Her follow-up question surprised me. She asked, "How do you feel about the man who hit you?"

Evidently, my answer surprised her even more. Honestly, the only thought I had was that the poor guy had just been in a horrible car accident on Christmas Eve, just like I had. How devastating it must have been for him to find out that someone had been killed. I simply said, "My heart goes out to him."

I knew he didn't hit us on purpose. It was an *accident*. He wasn't driving around looking for a way to kill my family. He didn't mean to hurt or kill *anyone*. And, even if he did, I was supposed to forgive him anyway.

The interviewer was caught completely off guard. She just sat there dumbfounded. I could tell from the expression on her face she was hoping I would elaborate. Although many believed that the other driver, Carlos, had lost much less than us, it seemed to me that his pain was just as great.

Uncomfortable with the awkward silence, I tried to explain: "His life is going to be impacted in even more ways than mine. He has to deal with the same three deaths that I do; only for him it's even worse because he has to live with the guilt of having caused them."

Carlos Prieto was on his way home from his cousin's house. He had been driving around, despondent, because the mother of his two-year-old son had threatened to leave him. I tried to imagine how sad he must have been. Then I thought of what it would be like for a twenty-four-year-old man to wake up on Christmas behind bars, away from his family, only to be told he was being charged with three counts of felony manslaughter for killing a woman and two children. I couldn't even imagine how his heart must ache.

The mother of Carlos's fiancée confirmed that, telling *Salt Lake Tribune* reporter, Stephen Hunt, "He's heartbroken. He's very remorseful. He knows he's ruined many lives, including his own."

I spoke about the many strange circumstances that led up to the accident. What were the odds that two vehicles would end up in the same place at the same time, especially at 2:30 in the morning? We were out at a time when we normally would have been in bed, everyone was sitting in different spots than usual, we were driving on a road we normally never traveled because Cheryl couldn't figure out how to get out of the parking lot. It all seemed very odd.

Thousands of people were out partying that night, and many probably drank a lot more than Carlos. Why did they make it home? And why didn't Carlos? If we had been just a tiny bit faster or slower or if I had not picked up that one last gift that I just *had* to buy, we never would have collided at all. If we had gone through the intersection just an eighth of a second faster, everyone in the front seat would have been alive and we would have died. If we had been an eighth of a second slower, no one would have died at all. Why was it them instead of us?

I thought about how, after literally years of promising to go to a recital, Ian had finally gone to watch Felicia Fuller dance *that very evening*, just before our cast party. Just a few hours before that, he had run into his old best friend, Ricky Dowse, after not having seen him for six months. I recalled how excited they were to see each other and how they laughed and hugged and gave each other high fives. I remembered the testimony Cheryl had born just the week before in church, when she went out of her way to thank the people who had befriended us when we moved into the neighborhood two years earlier. Cheryl, Ian, and Julianna had each been given all sorts of unusual opportunities to see and say good-bye to the people who meant the most to them. It almost started to feel *orchestrated*. Was Carlos really to blame or was he also a victim of circumstance? What if the accident was "meant to be"? Should Carlos then be given *credit*?

The interviewer lowered her notepad and stared at me as if she couldn't believe what she'd heard. She just couldn't fathom why I didn't hate him. But his race, immigration status, and alleged crimes didn't make any difference to me. To me they had little bearing on what happened to my family. I tried to clarify. "Suppose I'd been hit by a temple president who had a heart attack and ran a red light on his way home from a day of faithful service. My family would still be gone. Should I hate and vilify *him*?"

Anger and hate seemed pointless to me. Carlos's race was no reason to hate him. I served my mission with Latinos, so, if anything, that just made me care about him more. I knew he had broken the law, but the justice system would deal with that. They could condemn him if they chose, but I was required to forgive.

"He faces spending years without *his* family, just like I do. Plus, every day he will have to live with the haunting memory of what he has done; I really feel for him. I have hundreds of people coming to visit and thousands of people praying for me, but who's praying for *him*? That's the real tragedy."

I was astounded at how quickly the community began to react to those few simple statements. The nature and timing of our tragic loss and the simple way we forgave prompted many to spend that Christmas season doing more of what we should all do *every* Christmas—think about Jesus, the author and exemplar of forgiveness. In the Lord's Prayer, He taught us the importance of forgiveness; in the story of the woman caught in adultery, He set a great *example* of forgiveness; in the Garden of Gethsemane, He facilitated forgiveness, making it possible for each of us.

From the day the article came out, I began to be inundated with phone calls, letters, and e-mails, first from Utah, later from all over the country, and eventually from all over the world. Touched by our reaction, people burdened with anger and hate found their hearts softened. So many shared how the Spirit prompted them to then helped them forgive. They let go of old grudges, went back to church, forgave someone who had offended them, reconciled with their parent who had abused them, returned to their estranged wife, and so forth. Forgiveness became the focus of quite a number of newspaper articles, radio programs, and Internet blogs, and it was spoken of by families around their dinner tables.

One such family was that of a Salt Lake bishop named Chris Williams. When I met with him recently, he mentioned how he and his wife had been touched by our story. Although he had no way of knowing it at the time, Bishop Williams would soon join me in sorrow. On February 9, 2007, just forty days after our accident, he and his family were in horrible car accident that was hauntingly similar to ours. Cameron White, a seventeen-year-old boy from their neighborhood, driving drunk, smashed into his car, tragically killing his pregnant wife, Michelle; eleven-year-old son, Ben; and nine-year-old daughter, Anna. He wrote me a letter on May 25, just a few months after his accident:

> Dear Gary and family,
>
> I just wanted to write and express how so very impressed and touched I am for your example and the strength of your family, and how that has been such a support to me and my two sons. I also wanted to reach out to you and let you know you are in my thoughts and prayers. Although we've never met, I feel quite a bond with you and your family by virtue of the fact that me and my surviving sons are passing through such an incredibly similar experience that you and your children are going through. If anything I feel a little late in writing you as I'm sure our wives have already met and no doubt have started a good friendship. Besides, given the sometimes crushing nature of the holes in our lives, it couldn't hurt to have one more person to turn to, especially one that can relate on so many levels. . . . Your example of forgiveness has certainly helped me to continue to pray for, love, and desire healing in the life of the young man that hit our family. Thank you for your strength and courage![47]

Chris also forgave—before he was even pulled from his car. He said as much when he made his first statement to the media; then he issued an invitation to "all who have suffered, however unjustly, to lay down their burdens [at the feet of the Savior] and let it go."[48] I do not think it was a coincidence that the *Deseret News* article carrying his statement appeared the next morning, just below the lead story about a gunman who killed five people in a Salt Lake mall. The headlines truly belonged together:

*Mall Massacre*[49]

*Crash Victim Issues a Call for Forgiveness*[50]

In both Bishop Williams's accident and the mall shooting, Utahns were again confronted with a choice to condemn or forgive. In each case, the individuals involved and the community as a whole responded to those very public trials with Christlike forgiveness.

The year before our accidents, Chris and I each heard President Gordon B. Hinckley give a powerful talk on forgiveness. He spoke about how lives were changed when a teenager who had perpetrated a heinous crime was forgiven by the woman he victimized. Although neither of us consciously thought about that talk in our moment of distress, I'm sure it planted a seed in our hearts, like the Bible stories my mother taught me, the example my father showed, and the many things I learned from reading *The Miracle of Forgiveness* by President Spencer W. Kimball. I was so grateful all those seeds bore fruit and I could draw upon them when I was tested and it was time for me to choose. Forgiveness opened the door for the Spirit to free us from bitterness, anguish, and heartache. I was glad too that, in some small way, seeing how it did moved others like Chris to allow the Spirit to do the same for them.

Since then, Chris's own remarkable example of forgiveness has affected many more lives for good. He participated in the Forgiveness Project; he was filmed for a Mormon Message viewed by thousands on the Church's website and on YouTube; he wrote a book entitled *Let It Go*; and he provided that great example for the victims of the Trolley Square shootings, who in turn also found it in their hearts to forgive. Each time one of us suffered a public tragedy that year and forgave (i.e. me, Chris, the victims of the Trolley Square shooting, or several others referred to below in Elaine Jarvik's *Deseret News* article), it gave others strength to do the same. We never felt we were doing anything *special*; we were simply trying to do what was *right*. I don't think we even gave it any thought. We didn't have to; it was what we had been taught since we were children.

The year between December 2006 and December 2007 was filled with many amazingly similar stories that led *Deseret News* columnist Elaine Jarvik to call it "A Year of Forgiveness." On December 28, 2007, she wrote:

> Williams made headlines last February when he publicly forgave White. That was just six weeks after another grieving father, Gary Ceran, publicly forgave the drunken man who killed his wife and two of his children in a Taylorsville intersection on Christmas Eve 2006.
>
> In March, another grieving parent, Anna Kei'aho, stunned a courtroom full of onlookers when she forgave the man who had gunned down her son. In October, Ben Howard stood up in a Layton courtroom and requested leniency for the driver who slammed into his van on Highway 89, killing his wife and two of his children, a request that made the judge and court bailiff cry.[51]

After that amazing year filled with so many local stories of forgiveness, President James E. Faust referred to our stories and others, when he testified of the incredible healing power of forgiveness. He reminded us that the Lord requires us to forgive not just for the sake of those who have offended us but for our own good. He then quoted Orson F. Whitney, who warned that "hatred retards spiritual growth." Only when we forgive are we able to free our hearts of hatred and bitterness and to receive the Lord's soothing comfort and peace.[52]

When that talk was broadcast to millions of people around the world, many were able to draw strength from his words, and their lives too were richly blessed, as ours had been by President Hinckley's talk. And so it is, through small and simple things the Lord helps us all to learn, line upon line—from Him, from those He has chosen to lead, and even from one another.

Part of the great miracle of forgiveness is that it is contagious. As it spreads, it blesses the life of every person it touches—not only those who receive it, but those who offer it as well. Its reach is boundless. Like a pebble dropped in the water, its ripples seem to go on forever. Whether we are the ones blessed to offer or receive it, forgiveness is a gift that keeps on giving.

## 21
### Worth the Wait

As the sun began to rise on Christmas morning, children everywhere were rising right along with it and eagerly rushing to the door of their exhausted parents' bedroom. With bloodshot eyes and muted moans, parents dutifully dragged themselves out of bed and threw on their bathrobes as the children cheerfully gathered around them and shouted "Merry Christmas!" My Christmas morning couldn't have been more different. Although I had already been released from the hospital and was free to go home, I stayed to be close to my children. The blinds were closed, blocking out the light. Glancing at the clock, I was surprised I had been able to sleep so late, especially on Christmas morning. I stared at the door, half waiting for a knock, but it never came. Clarissa and Caleb were both still asleep in their rooms—not wearing the pajamas they would have normally opened the night before but hospital gowns. There was no sound of little ones scampering down the stairs, giggling, squealing, or tearing giftwrap; everything was still.

For some people that day would go on as usual, but not for us. The tree at home was dark. The presents still had not been opened; many never would be. Our celebration would be much more subdued. Nevertheless, there *was* reason to celebrate. For the first time since we were hit, Clarissa, Caleb, and I would all be together! Although it was difficult and immensely painful, Caleb had finally managed to walk up and down a flight of stairs. As soon as he passed his test, Caleb was wheeled over to Clarissa's room by Ben Ballesteros, the Children's Theatre sound and lighting tech, and his wife, Lacy. What a wonderful gift it was to be together again! We desperately needed to experience something familiar. All of us were suffering, but at least now we could suffer together.

Caleb was in a wheelchair and Clarissa was bedridden, unable to move her legs, but even so, as soon as we were together, Clarissa's room became our happy place. From then on, anyone who came to the hospital to visit *any* of us had to visit *all* of us, for we were always together in Clarissa's room. At one point it was so jam-packed with visitors—many of them bearing flowers, stuffed animals, and every imaginable kind of Christmas gift—that dozens of individuals and families were waiting outside the door in a line that went clear down the hall to the elevator. Feeling the love and concern of so many people gave us a glimpse into the joyful reunion we would someday have with our loved ones beyond the veil.

The following day was Clarissa's nineteenth birthday. The media begged for permission to come and see how we were doing, in hopes of providing anything positive they possibly could to a sympathetic community. When we finally relented and let them in, they were treated to far more hope and celebration than they or we ever anticipated.

Seeing the way Caleb and Clarissa strengthened each other was magical. Clarissa was able to sit up for the first time. She wanted so badly to be able to hold Caleb's hand.

Just before the reporters left, they were privileged to watch as Clarissa stood for the first time since the crash and then took two baby steps forward and back. We cheered and cried like she had won an Olympic marathon!

It would still be two more days, though, before she would be permitted to go home. Not only had her doctors insisted that she meet numerous physical benchmarks, they had imposed other requirements as well. Because she had been struggling much more than Caleb and I emotionally, hospital administrators wanted me to take her to meet with a social worker and grief counselor, which we did on December 28.

Those first days after the accident had been filled with intense feelings. Gratitude, grief, fear, and many other incredibly powerful emotions seemed to hit us each in waves. At our meeting with the grief counselor, those waves were like tsunamis. Clarissa and I were invited into an office just down the hall from Clarissa's hospital room. Two women, a social worker and a grief counselor, joined us, the first carrying a large brown box. I soon came to understand why both of them wanted to be there when we opened it. Although the first package I opened that Christmas looked plain on the outside, on the inside it was extraordinarily special.

The social worker sat the large moving-box on a chair and invited me to open it. "This box contains your family's personal effects—everything the police were able to salvage from the wreck."

Knowing what was in it made it extremely difficult to open, but I eventually rallied my courage, took a deep breath, and unfolded the flaps. From the level of my fear, you would have thought I was opening Pandora's box or the ark of the covenant! Obviously, opening it didn't release a swarm of evils or a legion of spirits, but in an eerily similar way, the notebooks, purses, and articles of clothing that had been left in the car all seemed to fuel flashbacks that haunted me in much the same way. Just as the modern-day penny in *Somewhere in Time* had done to Richard Collier, each object I looked at seemed to transport me to another place and time. Among the first things I saw were some of the last-minute presents I had purchased. Immediately, I was tormented by guilt. I knew we should have already been home asleep when we were hit. I felt like the accident was all my fault. Each pathetic trinket was a bitter reminder that I had traded what was most precious to me, my family, for a worthless mess of pottage. I had spent the last hours of Cheryl's life away from her, buying gifts that no one would ever see. I felt so short-sighted and foolish. If I had only set even *one* of those things back down, we would have never known that a drunk driver ever passed through that intersection. But I hadn't, and so I was left to feel as if I, myself, was actually the cause of all our suffering.

Perhaps the hardest things for me to look at were items from the Christmas Eve dinner we never ate. A broken box of giant pasta shells, a tub of ricotta cheese, and a large block of mozzarella had been thrown into a bag that was littered with small bits of shattered glass.

Our meeting with the counselors turned out to be rather brief, in part because the professionals who had been sent to help us were not familiar with our faith. They were not familiar with our religion, but more importantly they were not familiar with our *personal* faith—forged in the fires of so many previous trials. The women were both puzzled and fascinated by how well we were doing. It was evident that the gospel had provided us with coping tools that were far beyond anything they had learned in school. Being a trauma and grief counselor would be a hard job, but without the gospel, it would be much harder.

We graciously accepted the few words of comfort they had to offer, then we took a few moments to share a few of the doctrines and experiences that gave us strength. Although they couldn't fully appreciate *how* nor comprehend *why* we were okay, they knew that we were. We had chosen to let our lives be blessed by adversity, and we had learned from experience how to do so.

Before I closed the box, I glanced through it one more time. Like Pandora's Box, after the evils had all flown out of it, one thing remained—*hope*. I found *my* hope buried in the bottom of that box—oddly enough, in Cheryl's cell phone, which would soon become Caleb's. For years after the accident, Caleb chose not to change the greeting on the voice mail. The first time I dialed that familiar number, Caleb didn't answer. After three rings, it went to voice mail. Instead of hearing Caleb, I was shocked to hear the sweet melodic voice of my wife saying, "Hi, this is Cheryl Ceran. I'm so sorry I couldn't take your call right now. Please leave me a message, and I'll call you back as soon as I can. Thank you. Good-bye."

For months, whenever things got too hard for me to bear and my heart was aching for the companionship of my wife, I would dial that number as I had so many times before when Cheryl was alive, just to hear the beautiful, familiar sound of her voice. It reminded me that, even though she was away, she was still alive, and one day, reunited, we would look at our time apart as a brief moment.

I trust that Cheryl *will* call me "as soon as she can." It is a call I very much look forward to. I do not know when that call will come. Perhaps I will end up waiting quite a while. But whenever that blessed day arrives, I will surely say it was worth the wait.

# 22
## Home

For us, Christmas had slipped by quietly and largely unnoticed. From the moment we were hit, time seemed to stand still. After a strange five-day detour to the Twilight Zone, I was soon on my way "home" to celebrate "Christmas" with my "family." I put those words in quotes because neither home nor Christmas nor family would ever be the same.

After our appointment with the social worker and grief counselor, Clarissa went back to her room, where Caleb was waiting. She would still have to finish going through a lengthy discharge process with her nurse, change into street clothes, and supervise the handful of friends who were gathering the many gifts she had been given. Eventually she and Caleb would be helped to the car of our stake patriarch, Brother Hoffman, and his wife, who would bring them to our house. Meanwhile, Erol and I drove home ahead of them to try to prepare a belated Christmas.

As I gathered my things, including the box I had just been given, I suddenly found myself pondering how I was going to get home. I had almost forgotten that my only car was totaled. As if he were able to read my mind, Glenn Kimber walked up and stealthily slipped me the keys to a 4Runner, with a hushed, "You keep it as long as you need it, Brother."

As I struggled to find some way to thank him, Erol snuck up from behind me, put his arm around my shoulder, snatched the keys away, and wryly quipped, "Why don't you let *me* drive, Gar . . ."

That turned out to be a better idea than I realized. Being on the road was much harder than I thought it would be. Just being in a car was emotionally traumatic. Every time we approached a stoplight, if any vehicle to our right was still moving, I imagined it speeding through the light and hitting us. Although I was a passenger, I would panic and slam my foot into the floor, reaching for a nonexistent brake. When it failed to stop us, I would panic all the more. At every intersection I would have a flashback and relive the accident. Driving at night, I soon learned, was *worse*.

Noticing the frenzied look in my eye and determined to keep my spirits up, Erol did his best to distract me as we made our way home to Cedar Hills.

It was strange to drive home without my family. I felt empty. Everywhere I looked I saw wonderful things that had always made me happy, but I found they made me sad instead. They reminded me that those who had become so much a part of my life were no longer with me. The snow-covered mountains looked beautiful and majestic against the deep blue sky that day. It was such a gorgeous afternoon, and I wanted so badly to share it with my wife, but she was gone. Somehow, without my even noticing, we must have become *one* because I didn't feel like I had lost my best friend; I had lost a part of me.

We pulled off the freeway toward Alpine. I had driven that road many times in recent weeks. In some ways, driving on it almost made life feel "normal." For a moment it almost felt like the accident had only been a dream. I half expected to get home and find everyone sitting in the living room, waiting for me. I guess I must have been in that denial stage of grieving—it just didn't seem real to me that they could be *gone*. I have learned that trying to explain that feeling to someone who has never experienced it is virtually impossible, while explaining it to someone who *has* is totally unnecessary.

Erol pulled the car up into the driveway and came around to help me get out. Just seeing our house brought a certain sense of well-being. The yard was still blanketed in snow, just as it had been when we were all there together a few days earlier. I paused for a moment to survey the beautiful, steep white hills of the golf course behind our house. I could almost hear Ian's and Julianna's laughter in the wind as I remembered the wild and fearless sled rides we had taken down those slopes just a few days before. As I turned up the walkway and headed for the door, I saw that someone had tied three enormous white ribbons around the stone pillar on our porch. I immediately broke into tears, simultaneously grieving because of how much I loved and missed those who were gone and rejoicing because so many other people did as well. Struggling to contain my emotions, I walked up the front steps.

As I got to the top of the stairs, I noticed the wreath on our front door. It was the same one we had put up every Christmas for more than two decades. We had just celebrated our twenty-first anniversary a few weeks earlier. Memories came flooding into my mind too numerous and beautiful to even begin to describe. From the moment I gently swung open the door and stepped inside, everywhere I looked I saw something that wrenched my heart and triggered my tears—a souvenir from our anniversary date, a ticket stub from the Mormon Tabernacle Choir's Christmas concert, and on and on.

As I swung the door open, I noticed that the lamp on the sofa table in our large tile entry was still on, just as we had left it on our way out the door a few days before. Just beyond the entry, in the living room I could see the beautiful tree we had decorated together as a family. Ours wasn't the fancy kind with an elegant theme and elaborate matching ornaments; it was simple, old-fashioned, and wonderfully eclectic. There were ornaments that had hung on my family tree when I was just a little boy, many that Cheryl had made with the children, baby rattles, refrigerator magnets, stuffed animals, photographs, playbills—you name it. Each year we added some new, special decoration to remind us of the place we went on family vacation or some other special, life-changing event.

Beneath the glistening tinseled boughs were dozens of carefully chosen and beautifully wrapped presents, including many for those who were no longer with us. Unable to bear the grief of looking at them, and beginning to break down, I hurried past. As I did, I glanced up and noticed our little stuffed advent calendar.

Some of the Christmas traditions we honored were reading a Christmas book each night, singing a carol, delivering anonymous "twelve days of Christmas" gifts to neighbors, and discussing who we might give our Christmas jar to. Another was one involving that advent calendar. Each night after family prayer, we would gather together and watch as Julianna lovingly placed another small nativity figure on the calendar. I stared at it, thinking of Julie. As I scanned it, remembering each tender moment, I realized that all of the pieces were in place except one—the shining Star of Bethlehem. That wonderful sign, intended to point men to Christ, was the one Julie was supposed to put up on Christmas Eve. There it sat, still in its pouch. I reverently walked over to the calendar and reached out to put it in its place, but I just couldn't bring myself to do it.

"I'll leave it for Julie," I said to my brother.

For several years the star remained, untouched, in its pouch, to remind us of Julie. Now, each year we put it in its place over the stable to remind us of Jesus. It helps us remember that the sign *did* come, that *Jesus* came, and that, because of Him, one day we will all be together again.

I walked under the long swags of evergreen garland dressed in red bows into the kitchen and over to the fridge.

"Hey, E," I said, trying to mask my emotions, "do you want something to drink?"

As I looked at the refrigerator, I noticed a large picture that hung on the door. It had been taken just a few weeks earlier when Clarissa took "Jewels" to see Disney on Ice. The sight of their smiles and the thought of them no longer being together started me crying again.

"No thanks, Gar," Erol answered from the living room. Oblivious to the new instrument of torture I had discovered, he stood casually admiring our unusual tree. When he joined me a few minutes later, he caught me staring at the picture, one hand on Julie's face and the other wiping my eyes with a dish towel. I was crying like a baby. Embarrassed, I nervously tried to hide my emotions and explain away the tears. "I must be allergic to the dust on the fridge."

He walked over and silently put his arm around me.

Erol was usually as tough as nails. He never really aspired to be one of those kinder, gentler, man-of-steel-and-velvet type guys. But in those hours his heart was tender and full of compassion. He responded to my pain with sensitivity. He knew I hurt, and *his* heart was breaking too.

I walked down the long hallway that led to the master bedroom. On the easy chair beside the bed was the outfit Cheryl had hurriedly changed out of before heading to our last show at Hale. In the bathroom, Julie's Disney princess nightgown was lying on the vanity she had stood in front of while Cheryl lovingly fixed her hair. I picked up the brush I had used so often to stroke Cheryl's hair while we watched movies or when she was sad or stressed or overwhelmed. As I stood by the sink reminiscing about those wonderful times, the smell of her hand lotion made it seem like she was standing there. The void in my heart felt enormous! Everything seemed to remind me of her—a bottle of shampoo, a closet full of clothes, scriptures left open on the nightstand. Everything tugged at my heartstrings and made me miss her more.

I felt like a stranger in my own house. On the one hand, I felt a profound, almost palpable reverence, like I was walking through a sacred shrine. At the same time, there was something eerie and creepy about walking through a place full of stuff that belonged to dead people. But most unsettling of all was the silence.

The constant chatter of familiar voices was gone, and the lighthearted laughter of happy children had faded into oblivion. Everyday noises had fallen silent. There was no sound of running water or clanging pots at the kitchen sink, no buzzing clothes dryer, no ringing of cereal as it was poured into a bowl, no one playing beautiful music on the piano. There was nothing . . . absolutely *nothing*.

My house, my heart, and my life felt totally empty.

With my senses and emotions on overload, and feeling myself powerless to process any more memories or grief, I turned to walk out of the room. As I headed out, I stopped in the doorway and stared back blankly at our king-size bed. Suddenly I felt like a two-year-old. I couldn't bear the thought of sleeping alone! For more than a year, I would have Caleb sleep in Cheryl's spot. Whenever he was gone, it was terrible for me. I struggled with fear and loneliness. Sometimes I would cuddle my three-foot-tall stuffed dog or lay it on its side and cover it with blankets so it looked as if Cheryl was sleeping beside me. When I was alone, I usually slept with the lights on. I couldn't be in the house without uplifting music or movies playing. Often I would wake up to see that my movie had ended. Too uncomfortable with the silence, I would leave the DVD menu playing and just lie there and listen to the theme song play over and over again until I drifted off to sleep.

Everyone who heard about the accident knew that my life would never be the same. I was just barely beginning to understand why.

As I stood staring into my room, I thought about a "normal" day, realizing that, from then on, there wouldn't be anything *normal* about it. From the time I would roll over to turn off my alarm each morning to the time I got off my knees and crawled into bed at night, almost every significant part of my day was affected. My wife and children had been part of virtually everything I did. It amazed me how much of my happiness had come from the simple things we did together every day that we all took for granted. Suddenly there was no one to kiss me at the door or hold the other side of the hymn book in church. It was now always my turn to cook and always my turn to do the laundry. I did all the shopping . . . and driving . . . and teaching. I set, I cleared, I washed, I dried. The budget was mine, the bills were mine, the disciplining and all the problem solving were mine. I had to prepare every family home evening lesson and make sure we all made it to church on time with neat hair, pressed clothes, and matched socks.

Eventually we figured out how to create a new kind of "normal." Family prayers included three, not six. Recipes were cut in half. We even began to get used to the quiet. But there was one thing I never figured out—each day when I made my own lunch, I could never quite figure out how to surprise myself with love notes.

It seemed like the only things that really remained were Clarissa, Caleb, personal prayer, and scripture study. Not even they remained unchanged; all of them became far more important, more meaningful, and more loved.

"Hey, Gar, are you okay?" Erol asked, as he found me in my doorway, visibly shaken, still staring into my room.

Unable to speak, I nodded, but obviously I wasn't. I had barely been home for a half an hour, but I was already beginning to see that I had no idea how much my life had already changed.

Home just didn't feel like home.

# 23
## Christmas Would Never Be the Same

I WALKED BACK TO THE living room and sat down on the overstuffed love seat to try to gather myself. As I sat there, I happened to glance up at the railing on the winding staircase. There, on the bottom post, I saw a Santa hat like Ian's. I couldn't help but smile as I thought of it. He wore his everywhere at Christmas time. I sighed as I thought about how different my Christmases would be without him.

Christmas! With all my reminiscing, I had forgotten the whole reason we came home before the kids. We had very little time, and there was so much to do.

"Hey, Erol, can you come help me with this?" I called to my brother.

He had gone upstairs and was looking at drawings, swords, and the replica light saber in Ian's room. He came to the stairs and peeked over the railing. "Sure, what do you need?"

"Let's try and get all the presents for Cheryl, Ian, and Julianna out from under the tree."

Each gift was a stark reminder of what *wasn't*. I picked up the first one and started bawling. I told Erol, "If they do this to me, imagine the kids."

As we started going through the gifts, it seemed like just about every gift tag had one of their names either on the "to" or the "from" side. One by one, we pulled out the gifts that were "to" them. Meanwhile, the gifts that were *from* Cheryl, Ian, and Julianna were left by the tree. It would mean more to each of us to receive a gift from someone who was so far away.

I ran and put on the red-and-white striped nightshirt and cap that I traditionally wore on Christmas morning then scrambled around the house, trying to get everything ready. Thankfully, Santa had stuffed the stockings while we were gone, even though we hadn't left him any cookies. We lit some scented candles, turned on all the Christmas lights, lined up the stockings, and carefully arranged the presents.

About fifteen minutes before Caleb and Clarissa arrived, a KSL news crew showed up. I was so excited to see the kids that I barely knew the crew was there. While they worked to set up cameras and tripods, we rushed to turn on Christmas music and make all the last-minute preparations for our belated "Christmas morning." The news crew kept asking us if we were sure it was okay that they were there. It must have been a lot more awkward for them than for us. I appreciated how sensitive they were to the unique nature of our little "celebration." In the end, they respected both our time and privacy and didn't stay long. They knew how special that time would be for us. They just wanted to be there long enough to capture the incredible, happy moment when the kids got home and we could finally celebrate Christmas. And what a magnificent moment it was!

It broke people's hearts that, for us, Christmas was ruined forever. They figured that for the rest of our lives, the holiday season would be marred by sad memories, and it would become nothing more than an excruciatingly painful reminder of all we had lost. They lamented that Christmas would never be the same for us. Many who knew and loved us had even struggled to enjoy it themselves. It saddened them that a careless act could keep Christmas from ever coming to our house.

They didn't understand. That wasn't true at all!

As Dr. Seuss said so eloquently about the Grinch, "He didn't stop Christmas from coming; it came! Somehow or other, it came just the same!"[53]

And it was even more special than usual. Losing my wife, my son, and my daughter didn't *destroy* Christmas; it *sanctified* it. For us, Christmas that year was more focused than ever on Christ. We were so much more thankful that through His suffering in Gethsemane the Savior had born both our sins and our sorrows. We were so much more grateful that, by His death and Resurrection, He had provided us all with the hope and promise of eternal life. And we found that with a greater appreciation of those things, Jesus's birth meant more to us than ever.

Our stockings were brimming, the presents were amazing, the magic of Christmas was absolutely enchanting. But that year, because we were encircled about in the arms of His love as never before, we were reminded what Christmas was all about. The Grinch got it right: "Maybe Christmas, he thought, doesn't come from a store; Maybe Christmas—perhaps—means a little bit more. And what happened just then was, in Whoville, they say, That the Grinch's small heart grew three sizes that day."[54]

And so it was with us. Through adversity, our Father in Heaven had helped us develop a depth of feeling too glorious to describe. Sorrow had stretched our souls for joy. We came to know anguish and grief like we had never known before, but by knowing it we were also enabled to know greater joy, peace, comfort, hope, and gratitude than we ever had as well.

What most people suspected turned out to be true: Christmas would never be the same.

It would be *better*!

# 24
## An Unexpected Chance to Say Good-bye

THE NEXT MORNING THE PHONE rang; it was Joel Kelly. Moved by our heartache and by his own sorrow at the loss of little Julianna, Joel—a friend from Hale Theatre—had worked tirelessly to ease our burdens from the moment he heard about the accident. He did most of the paperwork to register us at the hospitals; he negotiated invoices and made sure my brother had a ride to the hospital; he notified family and friends of the accident, helped set up a donation account, coordinated with the media, researched insurance, brainstormed with Crime Victims Reparation, and made all of the funeral arrangements with the mortuary. In the hospital, he was at each of our bedsides or anywhere else we needed him to be. Joel had a message for me: "The mortuary called. They need you to go and pick out the caskets."

Erol drove me to the funeral home a few minutes away. The funeral director, Shawn Warenski, greeted us warmly and invited us to go downstairs. He was sensitive and kind and became a good friend. It is hard to describe what I felt as I walked around looking at all of the coffins. I was battling a torrent of tender, painful memories of the many loved ones I had already buried. Just four years earlier, we had buried our youngest son, Brayden, who had succumbed to cancer.

My brother Dennis had died of AIDS just four months later. Over the course of his illness, he lost three quarters of his body weight and dropped to just fifty-four pounds before he finally died. I saw him on a "good day" a few months before he passed away. Six feet tall and eighty-five pounds at that time, he looked like a prisoner from a concentration camp. Still, he was able to get up, dress, and carry on a conversation without too much pain. He was even able to smile a little. In the weeks that followed, he was literally reduced to skin and bones.

Mom passed away of a heart attack two months later, in August. She had only recently moved to a complex for seniors. When I found her, she had been lying dead on her sofa for seven days, with the air conditioning turned off. The sight and smell is unbearable to remember but impossible to forget. My father would die a year later of a stroke.

Each casket seemed to trigger some grim memory. Tiny ones reminded me of all the babies we had buried. Women's caskets elicited torturous recollections of my mother. Each one seemed to stir its own unique form of agony.

Eventually we stood before a beautiful white casket with copper handles, adorned with roses and a pastel-pink satin lining. The moment I saw it I knew it would be Julianna's. The funeral director confirmed that this particular one would be an appropriate size for a little girl of seven and a half. A few feet away I found another of mauve and silver, lined with an even more elegant pink satin. I chose that one for Cheryl. Finally I noticed a stately and masculine mahogany coffin lined in white. Its handles reminded me of Boromir's sword from *The Lord of the Rings*, which Ian loved. I couldn't think of a more appropriate resting place for a young man who would be buried holding the "sword of the king."

After picking out the caskets and vaults, I leaned against my brother, who hugged me in support. Then we followed the mortician up the stairs.

As we arrived back on the main floor, Shawn turned to look at me, and pointing to a room a few feet away, he said, "Your family is waiting in there. You can see them now." Then he paused for a moment and added, "They're not fully prepared yet, but I thought you might want to see them. Take as much time as you'd like."

His comment caught me totally off guard. It hadn't even occurred to me that they were actually *there*. In fact, I was so shocked I didn't even feel like I could go in to see them. My brother could see my distress, and he immediately came to my side to buoy me up.

"You don't have to go in if you don't want, Gar."

I thought for a moment then said, "No. I *need* to."

I took a deep breath to gather myself. Suddenly it was all so real. I didn't feel prepared. Even so, I turned and walked into the room. There, on three tables draped in linens, lay my wife, my son, and my daughter. I drew near them with a feeling of sacred reverence. As I looked first at Cheryl, then Ian, then Julie, my heart swelled with gratitude for an amazing tender mercy. When they were taken from the scene of the accident, I thought I would never see them again, but suddenly, there they were in front of me!

I had found my mother so long after her death that we had to have a closed casket. With no viewing, my brothers and I never really got to say good-bye. For some reason I believed it would be the same with these three. When they were all taken away after the accident, it felt as if they had been erased—like they had never existed at all. But now, as they lay before me, I felt as if these three beloved people who had been ripped out of my life had somehow been mercifully returned to the earth so I might say good-bye.

Only now that my eyes were blessed to see them again did I realize how powerfully I had felt their absence. My heart was so full! If only for a short time, they were with me again. My eyes filled with tears and my heart with gratitude as I gazed lovingly upon those three glorious faces.

I spent quite a while with them, trying my best to memorize every feature that I would only be favored to see for a short time more. Feeling them present, I spoke to them—not to the empty shell that lay on each table, but to the living spirits that I was sure lingered nearby. I reminisced about a lifetime of dreams and accomplishments, joys and sorrows, trials and victories. Each of their wonderful lives flashed before my eyes. Thousands of rapturous moments, poignant feelings, birthdays and laughter, singing and games raced through my mind.

I looked in awe at the expression of peace on each of their faces. They looked like they could just open their eyes. How I longed for the day when their eyes *would* open again and look back at me with glimmering light of life and love.

In that moment, I could not imagine how, in ten thousand lifetimes, I would ever recover from losing them.

I will always be grateful to Shawn Warenski for giving me that opportunity to see Cheryl, Ian, and Julianna, and I am grateful that he was able to make them look so natural. Their subtle smiles and sweet expressions of perfect peace brought unspeakable comfort to me. I knew they were in a far happier place, but it made it easier that they *looked* happy. Knowing of their joy removed the bitterness of their absence but not the pain of it. Like having a child on a mission, knowing where they were and that they were doing something good brought a measure of peace, but it certainly didn't make me miss them any less.

I stood and looked at Ian for a moment. It warmed my heart to see him wearing the self-same expression of blissful serenity he did when I had peered through the window and seen him sleeping in the car. I half believed that if I just reached out my hand and gave him a little nudge he would open his eyes, sit right up, and laugh about how he'd tricked me.

Without question, Ian's death was the hardest for me. Julianna had not yet turned eight. Our Church teaches that "children who die before they reach the age of accountability are saved in the celestial kingdom of heaven."[55] Cheryl, meanwhile, had lived a full life and was as pure and Christlike a person as I had ever known. If anyone had ever proven their faith, it was her. But the best part of Ian's life was just beginning. He had so much to live for! I was tortured by thoughts of what might have been and tormented because it should have been me in his place.

Of course we could spend an eternity asking "what if?" What if Carlos had gone home a different way or had hesitated somewhere just long enough to change a radio station? What if we had all been in our normal seats, or we had taken our normal route home? What if Ian, Julie, and I had died and Cheryl was left to endure the loss? Could she have ever borne that grief?

Clarissa told me something after the accident that gave me a hint. We were always very faithful about wearing our seat belts. Shortly before the accident, the belt on the passenger side had gotten so stuck that we couldn't free it. Since the passenger beside her couldn't be buckled, Cheryl refused to wear a belt as a driver. She insisted that if any of us were to die, she couldn't bear the loss, "so I'm just going to have to go with them."

If she had only been wearing her seat belt that night, she might still be with me today.

When I was done with my own personal viewing and had said my good-byes, Shawn invited me into his office. He told me a remarkable story of what happened when he was preparing their bodies. I was amazed as I tried to reconcile his experiences with my own. It filled me with wonder at the power of the mind and the mercy of God.

Right after the impact, I held Ian's head in my lap, looked right at his face, and began to give him a blessing, yet Shawn told me that Ian and Cheryl were both in such bad shape that neither of them should have been viewable. He said he had done nearly three hours of reconstruction on Ian's face alone. How is it that I could remember so many vivid details about the scene of the accident, and yet one that was so significant somehow did not register?

After the accident, Cheryl was facedown, and Julianna was underneath her. I never got to see either one. What I did know was that the hours that Mr. Warenski spent in preparing them—many of those hours being donated—allowed me to hold on to a lifetime of dear memories of my loved ones as I had known them in life.

Shawn told me as well of the experience he had while he was preparing Cheryl. With no pictures, he was struggling to know what she had looked like. While working on her, he happened to glance up at his monitor. Usually it scrolled through images from a security camera, but that night he had switched it over to its television setting. As he looked up, he saw a news report about our family. He had a powerful feeling come over him that he needed to do everything he could to help me. The station showed several photographs of Cheryl that gave him a clear picture of what he needed to do. The way he made them look whole was a miracle!

Like Shawn, many individuals rendered selfless service in countless ways, each one giving of their own unique talents. I am so grateful to all those who brought us meals, helped with laundry, cut our hair, surprised us with gifts, donated headstones, called to cheer us up, sent weekly cards and letters, e-mailed us, visited us, came to the funeral, loaned us their cars, taught my son, offered prayers, and so much more! May the good Lord reward each and every one of those selfless disciples of Christ for their love and sacrifice. And may He bless the kind and unassuming mortician who gave us a great gift—an unexpected chance to say good-bye.

# 25
## Three Imposing Caskets

I HADN'T EVEN ENTERED THE church before I sensed this would be one of the most overwhelming emotional and spiritual experiences of my life. It was still more than two hours before the funeral, but the massive parking lot was already overflowing and the line of friends and well-wishers wound halfway around the inside of the building and out the door. I saw friends and neighbors from long ago, some who had crossed the country to be there. Coworkers came from everywhere I had ever worked. I greeted friends and strangers of other faiths and people who hadn't worn a tie or set foot in a chapel for decades.

When we reached the Relief Society room where Cheryl, Ian, and Julianna lay in state, it was already packed with relatives as well as friends who had long been so dear to us that we considered them family. In the center of the room stood Elder Hartman Rector Jr. and President Thomas S. Monson of the First Presidency. The moment we walked into the room, an absolute silence immediately fell over the crowd, replacing muffled conversations with a sacred reverence and a palpable feeling of love and support. Before us was the harrowing and heart-wrenching image of three imposing caskets.

As I came upon the first coffin, I looked in and saw Julianna, my sweet little princess. With a black velvet dress, a beautiful updo, and a sparkling tiara, that's exactly what she looked like, a princess. Seeing her lying there in a coffin was more than I could bear. I turned to Caleb, who was behind me, and motioned for him to come and stand with me. Hugging each other, we just stood and stared in disbelief at the lifeless body of our sweet little Julie.

When we finally began to accept that she was gone, we walked quietly to the next casket. There lay Ian. Dressed all in white as if he were going to the temple, he looked handsome, happy, strong, and pure. On his tie he wore a pin with BYU's "block-Y" on it, and in his hands he held "the sword of the king."

Many wondered why Ian was buried with a sword in his hands. The one he wielded was one of his prized possessions. It was called Anduril, "the sword of the king." I felt it was appropriate because of the inscription engraved on it, which roughly translated to "Let the servants of the kingdom of evil flee me!"[56]

That was the motto by which Ian chose to live his life, nobly defending the right. Good and evil were ever before him, and he had learned to choose the good. Knowing that brought me tremendous peace.

President Monson and Elder Rector paid him a great tribute. Noticing that Ian was holding a sword, President Monson turned to Elder Rector and said, "Hartman, you served in the military, didn't you? Will you join me in a salute?"

Then those two great men turned toward Ian, stood at attention, and offered a salute. Since normal protocol dictates that it is the *junior* person's responsibility to initiate this courtesy, what they did was both a tremendous act of humility on their part and a very special honor for my son.

Struggling with my emotions, I shuffled reluctantly to the last casket. I knew I wasn't ready to say good-bye yet. There was Cheryl. Unable to even look at her at first, I stared at the wall in front of me. I took a deep breath and tried in vain to muster some courage. It felt like the very fabric of my heart was beginning to unravel. Desperately, I turned once again to Caleb for comfort. Drawing strength from his courage and perfect faith, I gazed with a broken heart on the face of my beloved wife and stared until I couldn't look any longer.

Clarissa was right behind and soon joined us beside Cheryl to greet the many wonderful people who were patiently waiting in line. After taking a few moments to greet family and friends, the doors were opened, and we began to greet and embrace the hundreds who had come to pay their respects.

Many came to offer comfort but went away feeling comforted instead. Being encircled about in the loving arms of both the seen and unseen, we felt an incredible peace that we tried to share. In our hearts burned a testimony of the reality of the Resurrection, and in our eyes was the light that came from a sure knowledge that our loved ones were not truly lost to us. We knew the separation of death was only temporary.

After two hours, the line still ran all the way down the hall of the stake center and outside. The doors to the Relief Society room had to be closed so that we, as a family, could pay our last respects and offer a family prayer. Clarissa and Caleb took turns pausing at each casket to say good-bye. Clarissa wasn't just in tremendous pain physically, she was also suffering emotionally. The look of shock in her eyes at the scene of the accident had been transformed into an equally tragic one of sadness and pain. Despite the many caring friends who stayed constantly by her side to lift and cheer her, she looked exhausted and forlorn. I watched as she lovingly visited with Julie and Ian, then as she bent over the casket of her precious mother and wept.

Cheryl hadn't only been her mother, teacher, stage manager, and idol, but she was Clarissa's best friend. No one meant more to Clarissa than Cheryl. The loss was unbearable.

When Clarissa was done, Caleb was given the same opportunity. Tenderly he moved from casket to casket. People marveled that, rather than being filled with mournful sorrow, his countenance shone with peaceful acceptance and innocent love as he paused by each person to simply say, "Good-bye for now."

His extraordinary strength and serenity were never more powerfully demonstrated than in the heart-wrenching moment when Caleb, just twelve, stood to say good-bye to Ian.

When Caleb finished it was my turn to say good-bye.

I cannot begin to share even the smallest part of what I whispered to Julie, Ian, and Cheryl. Suffice it to say that I told each one that I loved them and missed them. I made a solemn covenant to each one that I would always live my life in such a way as to merit their love and assure their eternal companionship. Then finally, with a broken heart and many tears, I bid each one farewell and prayed that whatever time remained before I joined them might pass quickly and seem but a small moment.

I spent a few minutes with my precious daughter then gently kissed her forehead and softly whispered, "I love you, Jewels."

I trudged over to the body of my son Ian and paused to reflect on the amazing, exemplary young man he had become. Softly, I placed my hand over his.

Finally, I drew near to Cheryl. It warmed my heart to see how sweetly she seemed to smile as she "slept." As my mind raced over the twenty-one happy years we had spent together, I was filled with a deep sense of gratitude for the privilege of sharing my life with a woman so selfless and angelic. I marveled at the incredible afflictions she had endured during her short life. If ever there was a witness that the trials and vicissitudes of this world can help us to become like God, her life was that testimony. She had proven herself faithful.

My heart swelled with sorrow but also with admiration and respect. I knew I was in the presence of a person who had truly lived an extraordinary life. It felt as if I were on holy ground. I reverently removed my shoes, walked softly to her casket, and knelt to pray.

After a few moments, I tried to rally my courage and find the strength to say good-bye. Knowing that in just a few moments the caskets would be closed and my mortal eyes would never again look upon the one who had been my strength and joy for so many years, I thanked her for the countless happy moments, apologized for all the times I had disappointed her, and promised to care for Clarissa and Caleb and do all that I could to lead them home. Then I held her one last time and tenderly whispered, "I love you, Bunny, and I always will."

When I was finally able to pull myself away from Cheryl, the funeral director began to close the caskets. Starting with Julianna's, he slowly lowered each lid, and we looked on their beautiful smiles for the last time.

The pain of watching their faces disappear for a lifetime was horrific, but there still burned in our hearts the bright hope—no, the *certainty*—that one day we would see them once again, greet each other with open arms, and rejoice together at the feet of our beloved Savior.

I wrapped my arms around Caleb and Clarissa. As I did, President Monson came over to us and began to speak. We all looked up in awe as he tenderly taught us. We quite literally looked up to him, for he is a giant of a man in every respect. Here was one of the Lord's special witnesses. It meant so much to us that a man with such great responsibilities would take time out of his incredibly busy schedule to come and personally provide such a visible show of support on behalf of the Lord and His Church. As my eyes met his, a sweet peace came over me. He knew how we were suffering. Clarissa looked up in anguish. His eyes seemed to gently answer, *Peace, be still.*[57]

Suddenly there was a great calm. For several moments President Monson taught and counseled us, offering soothing words of comfort and encouragement. He bore his special, apostolic witness of the Resurrected

Lord and the eternal nature of families; then he provided the one thing we needed most of all—love. He walked over and wrapped his massive arms around the three that remained of a family of eleven.

A few moments later, we knelt together, and I offered the family prayer. Among many things too numerous and sacred to mention, I thanked our loving Heavenly Father for those three blessed souls who had been taken home, and I pleaded for Him to help the three of us who remained to faithfully endure to the end.

When the prayer was over, we followed close behind as the coffins were wheeled down the long corridor that led to the chapel. Hundreds of people now filled the building, from the choir seats behind the pulpit all the way to the back of the cultural hall and onto the stage beyond. They all stood in respect and perfect reverence as President Monson, Elder Rector, and the rest of us made our way to our seats. Meanwhile, the funeral director and his associates carefully rolled each of the coffins into their appointed places. What a sight we must have been—a grieving husband and father flanked on either side by his two heartbroken children, seated in the gloomy, overwhelming shadow of three imposing caskets.

# 26
## Families Can Be Forever

I gratefully recognized that, as difficult as they always were, funerals were among the most uplifting and inspiring meetings I ever attended. They were not only filled with sweet expressions of hope but with heartfelt testimonies of faith in the Lord Jesus Christ and the blessings that come from His Atonement and Resurrection. The veil is often unusually thin, and the departed feel so conspicuously close that it becomes undeniable that the scores of loved ones gathered to comfort the grieving are not limited to those who are seen.

This funeral would certainly be no different. The music, much of which was provided by a huge choir of friends from Hale Theatre, was beautiful. The opening song, "In This Very Room," brought such an extraordinary spirit of love, joy, and peace that it felt as if the Lord might very well have been there.

The funeral was beautiful and uplifting—from the prayers and Erol's reading of the obituaries, to the touching tributes done by our former bishop, Greg Kofford, and Caleb's sweet, simple testimony. I listened intently, trying desperately to gather from them the strength I needed for my turn to speak. Another of the choir's songs, "We Can Be Together Forever Someday," written by Michael McLean, was one we found very comforting.

The reminder that families are eternal and that we will be able to be together again was certainly driven home when Clarissa spoke. Wearing a boot cast, Clarissa struggled to the podium. She knew she would not be able to stand for long. Leaning on the pulpit for support, she quickly shared a few thoughts and a poem. But then she did something that took everyone by surprise.

She and her brothers, Ian and Caleb, had been invited to go down to the Church's motion picture studio in Provo every three or four weeks to read and record magazines for the blind. At a separate viewing held the night before the funeral, the good sister who had been in charge of the project came to pay her respects. She handed us a packet of CDs that included all of the readings Ian had done. One talk was especially pertinent. Speaking of the CD on which Ian read that particular talk, Clarissa said, "I've brought it, and I'd really like to play it for you because it was the most comforting thing for me to hear."

She lifted to the microphone a small CD player and pressed play. The congregation gasped at the sound of Ian's voice. I couldn't hold back tears of both joy and grief as I heard his voice ring out in testimony over the loud speaker.

I broke into audible sobs at the sound of my son recounting a story written about the death of a young man's mother when the boy was Ian's age.

The story related how the author had gone home after the funeral, feeling totally brokenhearted. With an emptiness he thought would never heal, the young man fell on his bed, weeping uncontrollably. Between his sobs, he prayed out loud, asking God over and over again why his mother had to leave. Why did she have to be taken so soon?

My thoughts turned from Ian to Caleb, who sat by my side. He had every reason to be asking himself the very same questions.

With an aching heart, the young man in the story sought comfort in the quiet, soothing hymns of the Church.

I cried all the more. When music came from Ian and Caleb's room, it was often the sacred music of the Church. They loved listening to the Mormon Tabernacle Choir. Obviously they weren't your typical teenagers.

The recording continued, describing how the uplifting music had affected the boy: The overwhelming sadness and loneliness had suddenly given way to perfect peace. His emptiness and despondency were quelled. He carried that serenity to the chapel, where some of his relatives had gathered to mourn, many of them overcome with grief. They looked at him and marveled that he, her son, seemed to be handling the death so well.

I looked down the pew at the family that was all around me. My brother Erol was there with his wife and two daughters. On the other side were Cheryl's sister, Kaye, and her daughter, Meagan, along with

## He Can Heal

Cheryl's brother, Tom, and his wife, Sandi. As Ian read this man's description of his mother's funeral, it was as if he was describing the very setting in which we sat. There were many in the congregation who seemed to be looking at us in much the same way.

Ian's voice continued, recounting how the young man recognized the peace and calm as the influence of the Comforter. As it eased the pain, it bore a fervent witness that God and His Son live, that the Church was true, and that the sacred covenants his family had made were valid beyond the grave. With a fervor that increases whenever the veil is thinned, the boy committed to himself and God that he would live the way he knew he must in order to be with his mother again. In that moment, along with the comfort he felt, this young man had received an increased testimony, and his desire to serve a full-time mission grew.

My mind flashed back to an hour earlier. After looking at Ian for several moments, President Monson had approached me, put his hand on my shoulder, and said, "He is a missionary now and is doing a great work beyond the veil."

Ian's reading continued, sharing the boy's feeling that his mother would always be there to help him choose the right path.

Cheryl had always done that for Ian during his life and, sure enough, she *was* and forever *would be* there by his side to continue to do it beyond the veil.

Then Ian bore a powerful testimony that sounded like a trump in the ear of every person there. For this was the voice of one who was dead, speaking from the dust. With the deep conviction and the power of absolute certainty, Ian testified that he knew families could be together forever.[58]

What an incredible gift of comfort it was to hear those words. Clarissa then closed her talk by sharing what helped *her* in trying times, when others' faith might falter:

> I just want to bear my testimony to you that I know I will see all of my siblings, and my mother, again. I don't think I would be able to make it through this if I didn't know that. And I am so, so confident that they are happy. I can see it in their faces, and I can *feel* it.
>
> I've had such a tremendous amount of peace come over me, knowing how thrilled my mom is to be reunited with all of her other children again. And I really can't think

of anybody that was more ready than Ian. I hope he's writing music for the angels to sing up there. And Julianna died before the age of accountability, so she is right up there with all my other siblings. I know that they're happy and that as much as we miss them here, I know that they'll stay close and that they'll watch over us.

I'm so grateful for my dad and for Caleb and that they're able to stay here with me, too. I'm so grateful to all of you for the love and support you've shown. It means the world to me and my family. And I'm grateful for my Savior, and for His Atonement and the opportunity it provides me to be able to live with my family [again]. I know that families can be forever.

# 27
## Why

I WIPED MY EYES AS I slowly climbed the steps to the podium. After Clarissa's talk, Caleb had read some of the most beautiful words ever spoken by the risen Lord. Then he shared a sweet, simple testimony that touched every heart. I was overcome with emotion, but what filled my heart was not sadness but *gratitude*.

Clutching the pulpit, I looked out across a sea of faces. It warmed my heart to see how many people loved my family. I marveled that the hundreds I saw were a mere sampling of the many wonderful people who had shown us so much kindness. If there was anything that could possibly be done to help or cheer us, these good people had done it.

Just a month earlier, on Thanksgiving, I had prayed that the Lord would help me to know true gratitude. I never imagined this would be how He would answer that prayer.

I was so grateful for Cheryl, Ian, and Julianna, who were gone, and equally grateful for Clarissa and Caleb, who remained. I was thankful for the gospel of Jesus Christ, for His Atonement, and for the ordinances that made it possible for me to someday be with my family again. I was grateful that Cheryl and Ian had been taken so quickly and painlessly and that Julie had been unconscious so she didn't have to suffer. I was grateful that none of us had been in our usual places so the youngest three had not been left alone as orphans. And I was grateful that Cheryl didn't have to endure any more losses!

Spencer Simpson, a good friend from work, knew we had already lost five children. He understood our heartache because he had just recently lost a newborn daughter himself. Upon hearing about the accident, in shock and disbelief, he exclaimed, "When will the suffering end?"

I knew his question was rhetorical; still, I looked him straight in the eye and answered anyway, "For Cheryl, it just did."

Others struggled with a similar question—why?

Why would God allow something like this to happen, especially to a family who was trying so hard to love and serve Him? Why would a loving Father in Heaven allow a woman to be killed and her children to be left motherless? Why them? Why now? Why so young? Why on Christmas? Why? Why? Why?

The Lord's plan of salvation blesses us with an eternal perspective that provides the answers. President Kimball once spoke at the funeral of a young mother who had been similarly killed in a horrific accident. He asked rhetorically if the Lord could have prevented that terrible tragedy from happening. Of course he could. He is omnipotent! If He needed or wanted to, He could control every aspect of our lives. He could protect us from tragedies and natural disasters and shield us from worry, stress, illness, and pain. He could give us each a life of comfort and ease. He could make it so we never had to suffer. He could assure that the righteous were immediately blessed and the wicked immediately punished. And for that matter, He could even make it impossible for any of us to ever sin or make a mistake at all. Why, then, doesn't He? His plan was not to pamper us but to prove us. Satan's plan was to do everything for us. That would have defeated the very purpose of our coming here. Imagine what children would be like if they were spoiled and shielded from everything difficult. They would become completely dependent and utterly helpless. They would stagnate and never grow. And if the only option they were given was to do right, they could never truly prove themselves. Choosing the right would be a meaningless exercise that would merit no reward. Earth life would have accomplished nothing.

At the same funeral, President Kimball also pointed out that the length of a person's life is not the ultimate measuring stick of success. Life is more than just the here and now. When we see life as it truly is—a limitless eternal thing—we see that death is not an end, but merely a doorway that leads to another sphere of existence. Why did my loved ones die? Why does anyone? It is the way we are all made immortal and glorious. If properly understood, there is no tragedy in death itself, only in dying (or living) in sin.[59]

I tried my best to help the congregation understand that trials do not suggest that the Lord has abandoned us, forgotten us, or stopped loving us. To the contrary, "For whom the Lord *loveth*, He *chasteneth*."[60]

"Chasten" doesn't just mean to punish, but to make *chaste*—to purify, sanctify, and make holy. Why would we not want the Lord to bless us with something that could do that? Trials keep us in remembrance of God and how much we need Him, they force us to our knees and cause us to pray more often and more sincerely, they encourage us to evaluate our lives and covenant to be better. Through afflictions we develop a personal relationship with the Lord that cannot be forged in any other way. We truly come to know Him, and we learn how to be more like Him. How blind it would be to shake a fist at heaven and shout, "Why are you trying to make me more like you?" That is the very reason we are here!

"It is through sorrow and suffering, toil and tribulation that we gain the education we came here to acquire and which will make us more like our Father and Mother in heaven,"[61] Orson F. Whitney said.

Wilford Woodruff gently rebuked those who had that kind of something-for-nothing attitude when he said, "We have been called to pass through trials many times, and I do not think we should complain, because if we had no trials we should hardly feel at home in the other world in the company of prophets and apostles, who were sawn asunder, crucified, etc., for the word of God and testimony of Jesus Christ."[62]

As Charles Spurgeon put it, "There are no crown-wearers in heaven who were not cross-bearers here below."[63]

My voice faltered as I spoke of my wife. "When Cheryl was alive, people often marveled at how faithfully she endured so many different kinds of incredibly difficult types of suffering. They wondered why she would have to bear so much sorrow and why she would be willing to do it." I looked down at her casket and concluded, "The answer lies before you in the woman she became because of it."

Most of what we suffer in this life is the natural consequences of poor choices made by us or others around us. Of the exceptions, Henry Ward Beecher wrote, "There are many trials in life which do not seem to come from unwisdom or folly. They are silver arrows shot from the bow of God, and fixed inextricably in the quivering heart—they are meant to be borne—they were not meant, like snow or water, to melt as soon as they strike; but the moment an ill can be patiently borne it is disarmed of its poison, though not of its pain."[64]

I knew the pain of those silver arrows, but when I looked back across the years at my trials, I saw that the hardest times were always the ones when I grew the most and felt the closest to God. Through them all, "Why?" was never a pressing question; I had already been told why—"All these things shall give thee experience and be for thy good."[65]

Rather, what *I* wondered was why it was so hard for people to believe that Heavenly Father really loves us and wants what is best for us. Why is He given so much blame for what's bad in our lives and so little credit for what's good? Yes, sometimes life is hard. Sometimes it doesn't seem fair. But the rain falls on the just and the unjust, and bad things happen to everyone. Scriptural examples like Abel, Job, Abraham, Joseph, Moses, the Apostles, and Jesus Himself show that sometimes when we strive to do what is right, we find that, instead of receiving a reward, we suffer for it. It is often these experiences that make good people great. "For what glory is it, if, when ye be buffeted for your faults, ye shall take it patiently? But if, when ye do well, and suffer for it, ye take it patiently, this is acceptable with God."[66]

Some trials are awful medicines that our Father prescribes to make us better. It is up to us to trust His care, take each dose, face each challenge with courage, and never quit. Our life was full of trials, but as we tried to endure them well, the Lord taught us why we needed them.

Unfortunately, to some, "Why?" is not really a question at all. Rather, it is angrily shouted at heaven as more of an accusation. Too busy bitterly complaining about what they think is fair, they foolishly curse God and whine about His cruelty in the very hour when, if they were quietly pondering, they might be touched by His gentle and loving reply.

"Why?" must never be a *rhetorical* question or an exclamation of anger or mistrust. It is to be *asked,* humbly and sincerely, on our knees in sackcloth and ashes, with a heartfelt desire to listen to the answer. When "Why?" is softly whispered—with a question mark—it leads to relief from pain, peace amidst suffering, strength to endure, and understanding that grows into joy. When "Why!" is shouted—with an exclamation point—it raises the ire of a complaining spirit and leaves in its wake diminished faith, seething bitterness, and unnecessarily prolonged suffering. If we will humble ourselves, open our hearts, listen intently, and trust in God, He will help us learn *why*.

# 28
## Sweet Sorrow

To finish my talk, I had to address another question: "How on earth are you able to get through this?"

Being separated from my wife and children was horrible, and it would have been unbearable had we not known the separation was temporary. Clarissa, Caleb, and I all understood that Cheryl, Ian, and Julianna had not stopped *living*, they had merely stopped living *here*. What common sense suggested, the Spirit confirmed—they hadn't vanished into oblivion; they had simply moved from our company into the company of others.

A story I read many years ago helped me to understand that death is like a horizon. It is not the edge of a flat world where everything falls off and ceases to exist. "A horizon is nothing but the limit of our sight."[67] In *The Birth We Call Death*, I read the following story:

> In a beautiful blue lagoon on a clear day, a fine sailing ship spreads its brilliant white canvas in a fresh morning breeze and sails out to the open sea. We watch her glide away magnificently through the deep blue and gradually see her grow smaller and smaller as she nears the horizon. Finally, where the sea and sky meet, she slips silently from sight; and someone near me says, "There, she is gone!" Gone where? Gone from sight—that is all. She is still as large in mast and hull and sail, still just as able to bear her load. And we can be sure that, just as we say, "There, she is gone!" another on an even more beautiful distant shore says, "There . . . she comes!"[68]

As John Taylor said, "While we are mourning the loss of our friend, others are rejoicing to meet him behind the veil."[69]

One thing that helped us cope was knowing how happy Cheryl and the seven children who were with her must be. We knew they were alive and in a far better place. That didn't make us *miss* them any less, but it took the bitterness out of being apart.

As I contemplated all that Cheryl had been through and how faithfully she had endured it, I remembered the promise the Lord had made to another troubled heart, "Peace be unto thy soul; thine adversity and thine afflictions shall be but a small moment; and then, if thou endure it well, God shall exalt thee on high."[70]

Especially for the righteous, "Death is not extinguishing the light; it is putting out the lamp because the dawn has come."[71]

Sorrow comes hand in hand with the loss of a loved one, whether that loss is brought about by death, divorce, or waywardness, but "the only way to take the sorrow out of death is to take love out of life."[72]

We have been commanded to live in love and to weep for the loss of the companionship of those we cherish. Authors Paul Dunn and Richard Eyre explained what could allow for that sorrow to not be bitter but sweet. They told a story about two men who met on a long journey by train. Over several days the two became good friends. One morning one of them awoke to discover that the other was gone. Only then did he realize that he did not know the man's full name, his destination, where he had gotten off, why he was gone, or how to contact him. Not knowing if he would ever see his new friend again, the man felt sad, frustrated, bitter, and angry.

Just then a porter approached the man and told him that when his friend left during the night, he'd left a message. As it turns out, the man was in fact on his way to the very same destination to see his father. During the night, the friend received word that his father needed him right away, so he got off at the next stop and took a flight to get home sooner. The friend had left his number and encouraged the man to call him when he arrived so they could get together. That simple message turned the man's frustration to peace and his bitterness to joy. He was still sorry to miss the time they could have spent together, but knowing where his friend had gone and that they would see each other again soon, sorrow turned from bitter to sweet. The authors then summarized their analogy:

> The sorrow we taste with the loss of a loved one can be bitter or sweet, depending on one key ingredient—the

ingredient of knowledge; the simple, pure knowledge of our origin, our purpose, and our destination. The restored gospel gives us that knowledge. It tells us our origin; it reveals our purpose on earth; and it teaches us of the life hereafter, assuring us that loved ones will meet us there and that death is a temporary separation and not an utter loss. . . . Any dear possession, if separated from us for good purpose, and if returned in even better condition, produces joy rather than agony and peace rather than frustration.

One man loses his billfold containing a large sum of money. Another, with the same amount makes a planned investment. Both are now separated from their money, but one feels the bite and bitterness of permanent loss, while the other anticipates the day when he will retrieve his investment and enjoys the knowledge that it will probably grow in the meantime.[73]

Benjamin Franklin once said, "Our friend and we are invited abroad. . . . His chair was ready first, and he is gone before us. We could not all conveniently start together; and why should you and I be grieved at this, since we are soon to follow, and know where to find him?"[74]

There is comfort in understanding God's plan of happiness, but an eternal perspective is not meant to eliminate sorrow. It merely changes it from bitter to sweet, allowing it to coexist with faith, so we can be blessed by it. The key to our enduring every loss is to grieve with hope and know sweet sorrow.

## 29
## God Bless Us, Every One!

As President Monson stepped to the podium, everyone listened intently, wondering what words of wisdom and perspective he might share. Conspicuously, he looked from side to side at the dozens of huge, elaborate flower arrangements that occupied virtually every available space on the rostrum. Then he grinned and said, "My dear brothers and sisters, I think the pollen count in this building is the highest I've ever known!"

Everyone chuckled, even me. After spending so much time crying, it sure felt good to laugh!

President Monson's demeanor quickly changed to an expression of sympathy and compassion. He continued. "There are more handkerchiefs out; the Kleenexes are long gone. The tears are all right."

He looked down at the three of us for a moment before he spoke:

> I like what I read when I signed the little register in the foyer. "If there's a theater in heaven, the Cerans will grace the stage." How they grace the stage today. What testimonies we've heard! It should be easy for us to understand why the poet wrote, "It is better to come to the house of mourning than to the house of feasting. It is here we contemplate where we came from, why we are here, where we go."

Alluding to where we go, he shared with us a few words that he had whispered as he bid farewell to Ian:

> I said, as I leaned close, "You're on a mission in paradise, for thousands of others who need to hear your message." That's a real missionary farewell! That's what we've attended today—three missionary farewells, for they are alive, and they are real, and they're going to see loved ones

in their own family, and they've gone to see many others who've never heard the gospel of Jesus Christ. Can you think of anyone who is more prepared than those we honor today? I cannot.'

In words that would turn out to be more prophetic than we realized at the time, he assured us that peace and happiness awaited us just down the road. He also reminded us to what source we should look for comfort: "'Behold,' he said, 'I stand at the door and knock. If any man hear my voice and open the door, I will come in to him, and I will sup with him, and he with me.'[75] You and I are standing at that door."

He promised what would happen if we would accept the Savior's invitation: "Then, the tears will dry, and we'll realize that we've just said, 'So long, until we meet tomorrow.' Let us not forget this day! Let's remember how we felt—the tears we shed, the comfort we attempted to provide—and we'll feel better. But what's more, we'll *be* better."

What he said next caught me a little off guard. "There is nothing like a smile to replace a tear. Today is a day for smiling. The time for tears is past, and the time for smiling and looking to the future dawns."

Was the funeral of my wife and two of my children truly not a time for tears? I thought for a moment about who had suggested it and what he was. Then I considered who and what he knew, and I realized he was right. We had to allow faith to cheer our hearts and help us to keep moving forward. It was frightening to think of the lonely days that lay ahead, but I knew that one day my pain would ease. Someday I would eventually wind my way through the anguish and grief and find peace and happiness. But in that extremely difficult moment, I simply didn't know the way.

As if he had perceived my thoughts, President Monson quoted "The Gate of the Year," by Minnie Louise Haskins:

*Give me a light*
*That I may tread softly and safely into the unknown*
*And a voice said unto him,*
*'Go out into the darkness,*
*And put your hand in the hand of God,*
*For that to you is better than a light,*
*And surer than a known way.*'[76]

Then he went on. "This lovely family, the Ceran family, have cautioned us and taught us from their hearts and their souls, look to God and live. They've taught us to look at the Proverb—I think it's chapter 3, verses 5 and 6. 'Trust in the Lord with all thine heart and lean not unto thine own understanding. In all thy ways acknowledge Him and He shall direct thy paths.'"[77]

President Monson then pulled an envelope from his jacket pocket. With a broad smile, he said to the thousand people in attendance, "I have a letter from the First Presidency, addressed to Gary. Before he even reads it, he's going to *hear* it, in the presence of all these witnesses. You've heard of *three* witnesses; you've heard of *eight* witnesses. Well, this is the largest number of witnesses you've seen for a while!"

He then read the letter, in which the First Presidency offered their heartfelt sympathy at the passing of my wife and children. Words cannot express the peace that came from knowing they were praying for me. They assured me that, as husbands and fathers themselves, they understood my sorrow, but even beyond that, they testified, "The Savior knows the emptiness you feel . . . Let not your heart be troubled, neither let it be afraid . . . Peace I leave with you, my peace I give unto you. Not as world giveth give I unto you."[78]

After sharing many more beautiful words of comfort, they ended the letter: "Although there is no substitute for the physical presence and affection of your sweet wife and children, we pray you will receive the blessed assurance that Cheryl, Ian, and Julianna are happy, and once again with our Father in Heaven, who sent them to the earth for a period of mortal probation."

President Monson folded the letter, placed it lovingly back in the envelope, and handed it to me. Then he paused for a moment and recalled how he had gone to Hale Centre Theatre to see our play just a few evenings earlier.

"I like the words Gary spoke in *A Christmas Carol*. Bob Cratchit's wife asked, 'Was Tiny Tim a good boy in church today?' And Bob answered, 'As good as gold and better. He said coming home that he was glad that he was a cripple because it helped the others remember who it was that made lame men walk and blind men see.'"

President Monson concluded his message by pronouncing a remarkable Apostolic blessing. When he finished, we felt a great peace. We knew that the Lord's Spirit would be in our hearts and His angels round about us to bear us up.[79]

He ended with his special witness that Jesus is the Christ and with the words of a prayer that a small cripple boy, Tiny Tim, had once said, "God bless us, every one!"

# 30
## Everything's Going to Be Okay

HUNDREDS OF FRIENDS AND FAMILY members stood in solemn silence as the three caskets were wheeled out of the chapel to the west doors, where three hearses were lined up to receive them. As each casket arrived at the door, a half dozen or more pall bearers, each specifically chosen for the part they had played in that person's life, lined up to lift the casket into one of the cars for the long drive to the Valley View Memorial Cemetery.

When the procession arrived, the same pall bearers reverently removed the three coffins and placed them beside one another over the graves that would be their final resting place. Clarissa, Caleb, and I walked before them, hand in hand. When all three were finally in place, we stood by them and held each other. For a few brief moments, the six of us were all together for one last time, but we began to sense the reality and feel the weight of the imminent separation.

Eventually we were escorted to our seats, where we sat and quietly waited for the graveside ceremony to begin. It was overwhelming for everyone to see those coffins side by side like that, but for us it was even worse.

By the time the graveside service started, Clarissa was emotionally spent. Caleb, meanwhile, was handling things remarkably well. He wasn't just trying to be stoic; he was genuinely at peace. When I asked him why, he later confided that from the instant he first learned about the accident—a moment he referred to as "one of the most spiritual of [his] life"—he felt an extraordinary peace and a special comfort. When he received his patriarchal blessing, he was told the source of those feelings and he was promised that they would continue all the days of his life.

As for me, I had cried so many tears I didn't think any more could come, but somehow they just kept flowing.

There were many touching, tender moments during the ceremony, such as when the pall bearers each placed his lapel flower on the casket he had carried. For example, Ricky Dowse, who had been Ian's best friend for many years, had learned of his death when someone happened to glance at the front page of the newspaper on Christmas morning. He was devastated. Imagine how hard it must have been for a sixteen-year-old boy to go from a joyous reunion with his best friend just two days before Christmas to news of his death on Christmas morning!

It was even harder for Julianna's friends, who were mostly only seven or eight. Her very best friend, Ozma Richardson, had performed with her in a number of plays at the Children's Theatre. They were so adorable together—always laughing. The two sweet girls with bright eyes and beaming smiles had always been inseparable . . . until now. Dressed in a hooded blue velvet shawl, Ozma bravely approached Julie's casket and laid down a precious picture of the two of them hugging. In the picture, Julianna was wearing the very same tiara she wore in her coffin.

Watching that brokenhearted little girl at the grave of her best friend was more than I could bear. No matter how hard I tried, I simply couldn't fight back the tears.

When the service was over, the crowd and traffic eventually began to thin, and we had our first few moments of serenity and solitude. They seemed to bring a measure of relief. It had been an emotional day.

As the last few well-wishers headed for their cars, I stood and talked with Caleb. Several members of the media awkwardly waited in the background, determined not to intrude or disrupt the reverent mood. When they saw us finally preparing to leave, one of the reporters worked up the courage to approach us and politely inquire if she might ask a few simple questions. She knew that the public part of our trial was drawing to a close, but there was still one question that so many in the community wanted to ask: "So many people—hundreds of thousands—have been praying for you. More than anything, there's one thing they really want to know. How are you really doing?"

I tried to tell her that we were doing well, but she couldn't seem to understand how that was possible. The only way I could explain it was to share something I had said in my talk at the funeral, a quote from a Christian author named J. R. Miller: "The happiest, sweetest, tenderest homes are *not* those where there has been no sorrow, but those that have been overshadowed with grief, and where Christ's comfort was accepted.

The very memory of the sorrow is a gentle benediction that broods over the household, like the silence that comes after prayer. There is a blessing sent from God in every burden of sorrow."[80]

We talked about faith and eternal families. I described what it was like to tell Caleb about the accident and how he responded when he first learned of the deaths. Then I raved about what a rock he was, how much I depended on him, and what an incredible comfort he had been to me. She seemed skeptical at first. Everything just sounded too good to be true, but when she looked in Caleb's eyes, she saw serenity, light, and *joy*.

Knowing everything that we had just been through, she just stood there, amazed, and said, "You two are so strong! How do you do it?"

It wasn't about *us* or what *we* had done at all; what was amazing was what the *Lord* had done! One ancient prophet, who felt much the same, said: "I do not boast in my own strength, nor in my own wisdom; but behold, my joy is full, yea, my heart is brim with joy, and I will rejoice in my God. Yea, I know that I am nothing; as to my strength I am weak; therefore I will not boast of myself, but I will boast of my God, for in his strength I can do all things."[81]

Caleb nodded and then smiled. From that moment on, that became his favorite scripture.

I thought back to the words I had spoken as I pulled him from the wreckage. Ironically, it now seemed as if the tables were turned. As he hugged me, he seemed to say, "I love you, buddy. Everything's going to be okay."

# *31*
## Condemned and Forgiven

ON MAY 24, FIVE MONTHS to the day from the tragic Christmas Eve accident that had so dramatically altered each of our lives, Carlos Prieto and I would see each other face-to-face for the first time. Everyone knew how his actions had affected me and my family; it was time for a judge to determine how they would affect him and his.

I walked into the small room where Carlos's case was to be heard and sat beside Clarissa, who was already there. Several members of the media joined us on the right side of the courtroom. I looked across the narrow aisle that separated the twenty seats on our side from those on the opposite side, where Carlos's friends and family sat. We smiled a sort of sad, gracious, sympathetic smile at each other. Understanding our loss, they felt sorry for *us*, and anticipating theirs, we felt sorry for *them*.

It had been months since most of them had seen Carlos, and now they would only see him for a very short time. As soon as the brief sentencing was over, he would be taken away from them for years. It was so tragic, so senseless! Looking at all of them I realized that, even though they hadn't been in either vehicle, the accident had hurt them as well. Just like us, many of them were struggling to cope with shattered dreams, broken hearts, and injuries that would take years to heal, if they *ever* did.

Some of those I met were so burdened with shame they couldn't even look me in the eye. Some came over and expressed gratitude for the words of forgiveness they had heard in media interviews. Some just sat silently, overcome by the wretched gloom of what was about to happen. My heart ached for each one of them but especially for Carlos's fiancée and their two-year-old son. Christmas morning had come and gone in much the same way at their home as it had at ours, and they had surely shed as many tears as we had that day, probably more. Much of the characteristic joy and laughter of the day was surely replaced with emptiness, sadness, loneliness, and uncertainty, just as it had been for us. And, just as at our house, gifts for a loving spouse and parent had been left unwrapped—sobering reminders of what might have been. The mood in the courtroom and the tears in everyone's eyes made it clear that we understood each other's pain.

This court date had been long anticipated. Langdon Fisher, the prosecuting attorney from the district attorney's office, had informed me months earlier that I would be given the opportunity to share my feelings with the court. I was told that, in determining the nature and duration of a punishment, a judge will always give serious weight to the feelings expressed by the victims. Hurt and anger could easily lead someone to make emotional demands for retribution. But that was never my intent to begin with, and looking at his family, I had absolutely no desire at all for revenge.

The truth be told, I was barely even concerned about justice. What they chose to do with Carlos would have very little bearing on my life. My family was gone, and nothing the judge could do would change that. All I was hoping for was to look into the eyes of the man who done this. If I could see the pain of genuine remorse, that would be enough for me; there was no need to add to it the hurt of being hated and condemned.

So many people had reached out to offer me love and comfort, while so few had offered either to him. I felt sorry for him, and I wanted to ease his pain. I figured he and his family had already been suffering for months. Few people had a greater ability to ease his pain than I did, and I felt it was my duty to do it. Whatever the outcome of the sentencing—however long he would have to be behind bars—I hoped to make those years a little more bearable by letting him know we harbored no ill will. In my mind Carlos had already been punished for what he had done because his crime carried its own horrible consequences. Besides, if three funerals weren't enough to keep him from drinking and driving again, three consecutive five-year sentences certainly wouldn't do it either.

After a few minutes, the bailiff asked us all to rise as the judge was introduced and entered the courtroom. With a somewhat dispassionate and very businesslike demeanor, she bid us to be seated. Moments later, at her beckoning, guards escorted Carlos Prieto into the room, cuffed and chained. His navy-blue prison clothes resembled hospital scrubs. By his side was a tall Hispanic woman who was introduced as his interpreter.

At the appointed time, the judge asked the prosecution if they wanted to make a statement. Langdon told me to stand, state my name for the court, and make my feelings known. I read the following prepared message:

> Walking through a cemetery one is reminded that death is no respecter of persons. The causes vary that send our loved ones there, but the effect is still the same.
>
> Carlos Prieto—mi hermano (my brother)—has chosen to do the honorable and courageous thing in taking responsibility for his part in the tragic accident that took the lives of my wife of twenty-one years, my fifteen-year-old son, and my seven-year-old daughter. The law sees him as the cause, and this has led to somewhat of a public outcry. How ironic that as we who have the greatest reason to feel animosity toward him are striving to respond with love, we are, in the very act, vilified and condemned right along with him. Some who passionately oppose drinking and driving, some who staunchly oppose illegal immigration, and some who are merely twisted and embittered by prejudice or a cruel, calloused lust for revenge want Carlos to suffer as much as possible. Your Honor, I want you to know that I, and my children, who have been most injured by his actions, both physically and emotionally, harbor no such feelings. Carlos had no malicious intent. He wasn't trying to kill anyone. He didn't even have any intention of *hurting* anyone. He drank five beers and made a bad choice to get behind the wheel of a truck.
>
> No sentence imposed on him will bring those three back or make them live again. Like all of us, they *will* live again, but there is nothing that any of us can do here today to hasten that. All we can do is determine what punishment is appropriate for the crime.
>
> Experience has taught me that we are often punished as much *by* our crimes as we are *for* them. Carlos's punishment—the anguish he faces every day—has already been and will always seem to him to be severe. While

I have struggled with the thought of three lost lives, so has he. I know that he has felt my pain, and, in many ways, I believe that he has suffered much, much more than I have, having to live with the realization that he was the cause. Our greatest desire is that what happened on Christmas Eve will change his heart. We hope that he will learn from this and commit to himself, to you, Your Honor, and to us that he will never again drink and drive. And we hope that his story—our story—might inspire others to make better choices.

Carlos had five beers and made one bad decision at two o'clock in the morning. How many others had five beers that night? How many of those people even chose to drive? And how many more have made a poor decision at two o'clock in the morning, even when they were not impaired? The difference is that Carlos's mistake put him in the wrong place at the wrong time. In some ways he was a victim of fate and circumstance as we were.

Some people ask, "How much time should a man spend in prison for killing three people?" I wonder how different the answer would be if they asked, instead, "How much time should a man spend in prison for drinking five beers and making one bad decision?" Carlos's crime has caused a man to be separated from the woman he loves, and it has torn parent and child from each other's arms. It saddens me that his *punishment* will do the same. Hasn't there been enough suffering? Why should his two-year-old son be punished and not see his father until he is seventeen years old—if even then? If the demands of justice are the cause of such a separation, I wonder if mercy might not be given an equal voice.

I am overwhelmed at the responsibility and the burden that you bear each day, Your Honor, of having to weigh justice and mercy in the balance.

My wife taught our children forgiveness—both how to *seek* it and how to *offer* it. She used to read a scripture that says: "Wherefore, I say unto you that ye ought to forgive one another; for he that forgiveth not his brother his trespasses standeth condemned before the Lord; for there remaineth in Him the greater sin. I, the Lord will forgive whom I will forgive, but of you it is required to forgive all men. And ye ought to say in your hearts, let God judge between me and thee."[82]

I hold that certain judgments belong to man and certain ones belong to God. And I would not presume to counsel either. I rather acquiesce to each appointed judge to consider, in their own realm, all things with wisdom that far exceeds my own.

The district attorney's office has labored tirelessly in this case and has shown a tremendous sense of professionalism, helpfulness, sensitivity, and kindness in seeking justice, and in helping me and my children. They have opened my mind to the fact that you, Your Honor, must—in sentencing *anyone*—consider many factors, including the message a sentence sends and its value in deterring others from pursuing a similar course. I would not presume to put myself in your place. I only wish to make known our own personal feelings on the matter that they might be included when all is weighed together in the balance.

I am reminded of a valiant general (Captain Moroni) who surrounded an enemy (Zarahemna) who had ravaged his people. When, at length, his enemy was delivered into his hands and was completely at his mercy, he said, "We will not seek your blood." Instead of exacting vengeance, he made a different choice. He said, "We will spare your lives, if ye will go your way and come not again to war more against us."[83] Personally, that is all I ask. If Carlos will look me in the eye, shake my hand, and covenant that he will do all in his power to see that nothing like this ever happens again, that is enough for me.

I would hope that the thousands who are praying for *us* would also continue praying for *him* and that those who want to reach out and help us will also offer help to the woman he loves and his two-year-old son, who will be left without a provider. And I hope that his separation from them might, for *their* sake, as well as *his*, be as short as possible. Justice and other voices may demand what they will. But as for me and my house, what we ask for is an appropriate measure of mercy and leniency.

When I first began speaking, Carlos strained to lift his hands, cuffed and bound down with chains, to his eyes to wipe away the tears. Now we both just stood and wept openly. There was no shame in crying. The shame would have been warranted if we had *not* been moved to tears! Virtually everyone in the courtroom was crying, but no one more than Carlos and me—two heartbroken brothers.

Chris Williams experienced similar feelings. He too was eventually asked what sentence he thought would be appropriate for the young man who took half of *his* family. He described his feelings and mine so well when he said that, regardless of what was done in court, both he and the drunk driver had "already been handed a life sentence"[84] for they "both faced a drastically different—and uncertain—future."[85]

The drunk drivers who killed our families were accountable to society, and the law of the land demanded justice. Nevertheless, Chris and I were accountable to God, and the law of heaven demanded that those men be given mercy. And so it was that the men who had taken our respective families each left their sentencing overwhelmed by the feeling that they were, at the same time, both condemned and forgiven.

# 32
## An Attribute of the Strong

In a few moments the judge gave Carlos the opportunity to make a statement of his own. The broken man wasn't inclined to even defend himself. Instead, he showed where his heart really was. Through his interpreter, he said, "With all my heart, I want to thank this wonderful man who has forgiven me. I wish I could do something to heal his pain, to heal his heart. There is not a time that I don't think about it. I want to thank this man and his family for their love and forgiveness. But I cannot accept it because I do not deserve it."

Then, after I had just spent so much time pleading for a *lighter* sentence, Carlos told the judge that he deserved a *stiffer* one! In words that none of us will ever forget, he lifted his head, which had been hung in shame, looked the judge right in the eye, and said, "I would gladly give my *life*, if it would return this man's family or his happiness."

The courtroom sat in stunned silence. The only sound was that of sniffles and sobs from people on *both* sides of the aisle. What all of us were witnessing was repentance and forgiveness changing a heart right before our eyes. And because of it, all of us were changed as well.

As a member of a stake high council, I had seen men appear to answer for their sins. I had heard them confess and had wept with them as they poured out their hearts and faced the consequences of their actions, at times even losing their membership in the Church. I had also seen several come back later with a new heart and a renewed light in their countenance. In a similar way, I was privileged to baptize my own mother back into the Church when I was sixteen. I will never forget how different she looked rising out of the water than she did going in. But I have *never* felt a greater spirit of contrition, heartfelt sorrow, and remorse of conscience than I did that day in that tiny courtroom from Carlos.

When the prosecuting attorney stood to make a closing statement, he said that he had prosecuted many, many DUI cases, but in all his years, he had never needed to ask for a stiffer sentence than what was demanded by a victim . . . until now. He then made a case for the maximum punishment allowed by the law, saying, "Society has an interest in what is done beyond the feelings of the victims."

After a brief recess, the judge returned to the courtroom and announced her decision. Carlos was given five years for each of the three counts of vehicular homicide for which he had been charged and convicted. But citing the remorse of the defendant and the request of the victims, she decided to allow one of the sentences to run concurrently. His punishment was reduced from a maximum of fifteen years to a maximum of ten, after which he was to be deported and sent back to his native Mexico.

Part of the sentence imposed by the court stipulated that Carlos write a letter of apology. With the help of an interpreter, he had already done so. The text of his letter may help you to understand why it was that it never crossed my mind to hate him or to hold a grudge against him:

> My name is Carlos Prieto and it has taken me some time to be able to finish this letter. It seems to me that no matter how hard I try I cannot seem to come up with the words that heal all of the damage I have caused.
>
> I want to start by saying that I am so very sorry—that I feel so bad for what happened, and I do understand what you and your family are going through. I know what I did. It was a mistake to get behind the steering wheel under the condition I was in. It was inhuman and unacceptable because I hurt you and I broke many hearts. I did not see the consequences of my actions—hurting innocent people, breaking their illusions and dreams without right or reason. I want to let you know how regretful I am, and I promise you that I never wanted to do it and give someone a bitter pain like this. I never meant to hurt you or your family. It was my irresponsibility, and that is why I regret what I did so deeply.
>
> I feel so much hurt, sadness, and pain as it was never my intent that someone else's life would be taken because of my actions. I have been in jail for three months now

without drink, and I wish I could change this three months and the accident right now. I don't feel that I deserve all the love and forgiveness that you have offered to me. I wish I could have met you before under different circumstances. Please believe me that I never meant for this to happen.

I would give my life for you to have your family back again and to be happy. I know that is not possible, though I wish it was. I wish, the way it happened, we could fix it, as it was one second that changed our lives. Let me say that better . . . I changed your lives because of my stupidity and I cannot restore all of your lives.

I understand because I also have a family. I have a wife and a son, who I love with my whole heart. I think about all of the pain I have caused them also. It is so crazy how many people I have hurt. I know it is all in my hands and the answer was, "Don't drink and drive!" It hurts me because I did it, and the guilt I feel I will never forget. I would understand if you and your family hated me, but I also know that you don't feel that way. I appreciate it, but I don't deserve it. God bless you.

I let the alcohol control me, and I didn't control my sense that night. I feel so horrible, sad, and hurt too. There are so many feelings running in my head and in my heart every day. It's my fault, and maybe you can understand me too. I think about my own family I've left alone, without support, without my love, without protection, with their broken hearts too, and it's all my fault.

I think about what my own son is going to say about me. Maybe he will hate me. He is just two years old, but he'll grow up alone, and it scares me.

I hope all your family can forgive me. I want to apologize for everything. I don't know how or in what way, but please let your children know I'm sorry for taking someone away from their lives. I know you forgive me already. My heart is broken; my soul is empty. I have to face up to a new life. You are all really good people, with sweet hearts, and I thank you. I know it doesn't matter how many times I do apologize, it doesn't fix everything, but I will always be sorry. I'm so sorry!

I don't have any idea how I am going to make a new life, because there won't be a day that I won't think about what I did. I only hope and pray that in time all of your wounds may be healed. Maybe someday I may be able to tell you in person how sorry I am. I owe you and your family more than I know how to return.

All I can do now is thank you for your forgiveness and tell you my bleeding, aching heart goes out to all of you. I pray that God will keep you safe and help you heal.

Very Sincerely, Carlos R. Prieto

Why would people think it was so strange that I would ask, "Who's praying for *him*?" The whole time, Carlos, who truly is my brother, had been praying for *me*.

As we left the courtroom that day, the scene was very different from what anyone expected. His family was hugging my family, all of us in tears of compassion for the others, all of us victims of the same brief moment of flawed judgment that would dramatically alter the rest of our lives.

*Everyone's* burden was lifted because of forgiveness. Rather than dozens of adversaries leaving the courtroom fuming with bitter hatred for one another, we all left not only as friends but as brothers and sisters. As we did I pondered a verse: "For with what judgment ye judge, ye shall be judged: and with what measure ye mete, it shall be measured to you again."[86] I had no desire to condemn Carlos, nor would I dare, for by doing it I would also be condemning myself.

At Christmastime in 2008, I drove to the prison in Gunnison where Carlos was being held. He looked slender and bright-eyed and was doing as well as could be expected. To put him more at ease, I spoke to him in Spanish; to put *me* more at ease, he answered in English, which he had learned while there in prison. We were both so grateful for the chance to talk face-to-face. For so long, he had wanted nothing more than to look me in the eye and tell me he was sorry. And I wanted nothing more than to tell him that I forgave him. We spoke about the accident and about what we had each experienced that night; then, in a quiet moment Carlos thanked me for pleading with the judge for a lighter sentence. He thanked my family for forgiving him. And he explained how it was only when he was offered forgiveness that he was finally able to extend it to the person who killed his father many years earlier. He spoke of what it felt like to finally be free of the bitterness and hatred he had held inside for so long. Knowing that he had been forgiven allowed him to feel God's love, which rid his mind of the anger that had plagued him and the hate that had poisoned him.

Forgiveness is a wondrous, eternal round. Only as we forgive are we able to be forgiven, and only as we experience the joy and purity of complete forgiveness can we truly and fully forgive. Carlos and I learned the same powerful lessons as we experienced the miraculous way in which the Lord was able to purify, restore, and heal.[87]

Forgiving is not forgetting; it is letting go of the hurt. It eases our suffering and frees our souls, whether we are the ones being forgiven or the ones forgiving others.

Jesus taught us to treat each other with greater love. "Ye have heard that it hath been said, 'An eye for an eye, and a tooth for a tooth,' but I say unto you . . . whosoever shall smite thee on thy right cheek, turn to him the other also . . . Love your enemies, bless them that curse you, do good to them that hate you, and pray for them which despitefully use you, and persecute you."[88]

The blessings that came from trying were amazing.

Some were angry at Carlos and me for the way we responded to each other and said we were foolish and weak, but we thought otherwise. I told Carlos it takes a strong person to say they are sorry, and he told me that it takes an even stronger one to forgive. He learned that when *he* forgave another. Perhaps Ghandi said it best: "The weak can never forgive . . . Forgiveness is an attribute of the strong."

# 33
## Till We Meet Again

It was hard for us to live in the same house without all of the same people. Familiar places felt painfully empty without familiar faces. Day after day I was surrounded by reminders of those whose love had brightened my days. Those memories both tortured and sustained me.

A trauma expert told me that the best way to help Clarissa and Caleb heal was to have a quick return to normalcy. That was easier said than done. One thing that we found helped was having them go back to the Salt Lake Children's Theatre to perform. The owners, Tom and Joann Parker, treated the two of them as if they had been their own grandchildren. Being in plays allowed Clarissa and Caleb to be surrounded by dozens of friends who knew and loved them—and those who had died. They too were grieving. Somehow being together helped *everyone* feel better.

It was *horrible* trying to figure out what to do with all their things. I obviously didn't have a huge personal need for a Go-Go My Walking Pup or a dance outfit for a seven-year-old girl, but it felt *terrible* to think of dropping them off at a secondhand store. It felt like, somehow, doing that would be disrespecting them or trivializing things that had really mattered to them. I tried to give as much as I possibly could to their friends, though some things were so full of special memories that I just couldn't seem to let go of them. I filled close to a dozen Rubbermaid totes with clothes and memorabilia that were just too hard to part with.

What do you do with the Disney princess nightgown that your seven-year-old daughter was wearing when she hugged you the night before she died? What about the sweater your son just wore to seminary or the Santa hat he wore every day at Christmas time—including when, laughing and singing carols, you all gathered as a big, happy family to decorate the tree? Seriously, what do you *do* with them? Do you keep every notebook, tie, or bottle of perfume? And what do you do with a *wedding dress*?!

Many things that had always seemed so ordinary were suddenly transformed into priceless treasures. The sadness and heartache were almost unbearable as I looked through everything they had written, drawn, used, or owned. The clothes in their closets, the papers in their drawers, *anything* with their handwriting on it, even the markings in their scriptures tortured me. The day he was killed, for example, Ian had been studying about where people go when they die. The last verses he'd read said,

> Now, concerning the state of the soul between death and the resurrection—Behold, it has been made known unto me by an angel, that the spirits of all men, as soon as they are departed from this mortal body, yea, the spirits of all men, whether they be good or evil, are taken home to that God who gave them life.
>
> And then shall it come to pass, that the spirits of those who are righteous are received into a state of happiness, which is called paradise, a state of rest, a state of peace, where they shall rest from all their troubles and from all care, and sorrow.[89]

I was comforted to know that they were happy, but my heart still ached because they were gone. It hurt every time I saw my wife's name on a utility bill or, even worse, on an invoice from the hospital. And it hurt when I found the secret treasures each had stashed away in special places. In death, each of their flaws completely disappeared, while somehow all of mine felt like they were magnified a hundredfold.

I looked at their calendars and saw their plans. I read their journals and learned all about their goals and dreams. I stared at their pictures for hours and cried for days as I thought about what might have been.

But slowly, my children and I began to grow accustomed to our new life. As time crept forward, we gradually found ourselves able to laugh more and more. We began developing new routines and habits. We *had* to. For example, right after the accident when I cooked dinner, we would clear the table and take our plates to the sink—as we always had—but when we woke up for breakfast, they would still be there. We weren't used to actually *washing* them. The lunches that had always been prepared and left on the counter for us with a little love note were no longer there. The laundry didn't mysteriously just do itself anymore. Family home evening suddenly required a lot more work. We had always *helped* with all of those things, but now we had to do them all on our own.

Holidays and milestones were unbearable at first. But over time they too became less painful.

As Valentine's Day approached it occurred to me that I still hadn't taken down the Christmas decorations. Like the clock in our car, time itself seemed to have stopped on Christmas Eve. One day, while Clarissa and Caleb were away, I decided to go through the pain of putting everything away. I took the wreath off the front door as well as the ones that had hung on the lights on the porch and garage. Inside, I removed the evergreen garland that had been wrapped around all the railings then took down the swags that hung over the archway to the dining room. Tapestries, pictures, stockings, and twinkle lights all soon followed. Last of all it was time to take down the tree.

I put on some music to keep the mood festive—Christmas music at first, of course. The disk we had listened to when we decorated the tree was still in the CD player. I turned it on and started to lovingly remove each of the ornaments. For the next hour, I smiled, laughed, and cried as I unhooked and carefully stored each and every memory. Every so often I would change the CD. At one point I put in a Mormon Tabernacle Choir CD entitled *Love Is Spoken Here* and literally wept through every single song as it played.

As with most of the Tabernacle Choir's music, that CD created an incredibly beautiful spirit in our home. But it was especially powerful and meaningful because this particular one was all about the family. The first track, which we had often sung with our children, was a wonderful song entitled "Love Is Spoken Here." I wept as I thought of my sweet wife kneeling with us every day. I missed hearing her pray for us. It had truly quieted all our fears. The thought reminded me of 3 Nephi 17, which Caleb at read at the funeral. Each time she prayed, we felt like the Nephites who heard Jesus pray for them: "And no tongue can speak, neither can there be written by any man, neither can the hearts of men conceive so great and marvelous things as we both saw and heard Jesus speak; and no one can conceive of the joy which filled our souls at the time we heard him pray for us unto the Father."[90]

Cheryl was such a soft-spoken peacemaker. When we were first married, she made a cross-stitch that said, "Love Is Spoken Here." On the day she died, it still hung in our entry, beside our front door.

Several of the songs seemed to bring back similar fond memories. A few of them were favorites of those who had died. Others were ones we regularly sang in family home evening each week. Some just had lyrics or a melody or mood that invited reflection. Listening to that music as I took down the decorations by myself that we had put up together was torturous.

Eventually the CD played Harry Belafonte's song, "Turn Around." The sentimental and nostalgic mood of it had always brought me to tears, but never more than now. I thought of my sweet little girl, Julianna, and the miracle that brought her to us. Suddenly she was two, then four, then—all at once—I turned around and she was gone. I cried as I thought of all the things I would never see her do.

Eventually, just one ornament remained on the tree. I couldn't bring myself to take it down. It held a family picture we had taken with my mother in 1999. Since it showed all of us together, I had left it for the very end. It just felt wrong to put it in a box. It felt like some kind of unexpected, premature closure and awful finality that I was unprepared for.

As the last beautiful song played, I stared at the picture and wept. I knew that, somewhere, she and my children and many others were surely praying that we would find happiness, comfort, and peace; that our troubles would be small and our blessings would be great. It was almost as if Cheryl were singing the lyrics. "May the Good Lord Bless and Keep You till We Meet Again."[91]

As I stared at Cheryl's soul-soothing smile in that picture, I imagined what it would be like if I were blessed to see her one last time. I felt sure she would say exactly what the song did. She loved us and wanted us to be happy. In my mind's eye, I could almost see her gathering around her our seven children who were with her and praying with them that our burdens might be made light.

If anyone understood how our lives could be blessed by adversity, it was Cheryl. She knew, as I did, that after an incredible trial like the one we had just gone through, our merciful Father in Heaven would probably grant us some brief period when I would be able to walk in the sunlight. But I also knew that beyond that short period of rest some other trial was surely lurking. That's how life is, and that is all right, for it is part of life's purpose. How grateful I was that we had learned to both look for and find life's silver linings. That optimism allowed us to keep moving forward with confidence. We knew that behind every dark cloud and beyond every frightening storm of life, the sun really was always shining. Although it took a while to learn, over time we came to know that whenever a trial ended, we would always eventually be blessed to actually see the sun shining.

I can't explain what happens musically in the song. In layman's terms, the notes played by the violins seem to gently rise, creating an unmistakable sense of ascension. As the song ended, I felt chills racing up my spine and love surrounding me in a beautiful, rapturous way. I literally felt as if Cheryl wrapped her arms around me to say good-bye. Then I literally felt that her spirit let go of me and began to rise. As she ascended, I could feel her growing more and more distant until I could tell that she was gone. The presence I had felt was no longer there.

Suddenly she was gone—yet not just as she had been before. It was *different*. I realized that for nearly two months it had often felt as if she were in the next room. Many times I felt all three of them close—at church, in the temple, during family prayers—but in that very special moment I felt the same sense of absence I had years before when my son Jordan passed away. In an instant, she was just gone.

As the Spirit poured over me, I was filled with indescribable peace—a peace that surpassed all understanding—and a pure and perfect love that words are simply inadequate to describe. This amazing, special feeling of perfect peace and perfect love is the miracle that allows each of us to not only endure but embrace what we never could without the comforting influence of the Spirit.

I played the song again and again, savoring the sweet pain as I seared the memory into my mind. That rich, exquisite, soul-stretching, mentoring pain had become as faithful a companion to me as Cheryl had. I *wanted* to believe that there would be sweet tomorrows, but I was still haunted by thoughts of what might have been. Somehow, I would have to find a way to let go of that regret.

Julie was young and could rely on grace. Cheryl had lived a full and wonderful life, and clearly, she had proven herself. Because of those things, I was somehow more able to cope with their deaths. But I had struggled mightily with losing Ian. I knew he was faithful and good, and that brought me consolation. But for a very long time, I wept—and wept *sorely*—whenever I thought of Ian and heard the words *what might have been.*

There were times when I felt the message of that treasured song was as personalized to me as if Cheryl had written it for me: "Oh, Gary, I know it hurts, but the time has come and I have to go. Fill your dreams, my beloved, with sweet tomorrows. The future is so much brighter and closer than you know! Don't worry about us; we are where we belong. And never mind what might have been. Things are as they *should* be. I'm sorry, but I have to move on now and so do you. Never forget, we are always near you. And always remember, you are in our prayers!"

I bawled and sobbed and pleaded with all my heart that she wouldn't go, but she *had* to. When she finally left, my heart was pierced to the very center. She seemed to repeat the same words she'd said right before she died, "I love you, sweetie."

As I felt her drift farther and farther away, I believe that Cheryl, Ian, Julianna, and I all uttered the same loving prayer: "May the Lord bless you till we meet again."

# 34
## Stumbling Forward

SUDDENLY FEELING COMPLETELY ALONE, I finished taking down the rest of the decorations. I felt empty, lonely, frightened, and overwhelmed. But I knew I had to find some way to move forward with courage before the Lord could perform a miracle. He couldn't guide my footsteps until I was willing to move my feet. I knew things were going to be hard. Even so, I was determined to go on.

I was hopeful but at the same time clueless. I didn't have any idea what I was going to do or how I was going to do it. How could I go back to work and leave my kids alone, and yet how would I pay off hundreds of thousands of dollars in medical bills if I didn't? How could I possibly homeschool Caleb if I had to be at work all day, and yet how could I ever face Cheryl if I didn't? And how would I help Clarissa with college?

To help her cope, Clarissa decided to distract and busy herself with a job. She was working far from home, and we only had one vehicle. She didn't like having to ask for rides, and it was even harder for her when I wasn't around to give them. Eventually she started to talk about moving. She found it difficult, emotionally, to be at the house anyway. It was growing harder and harder for her to stay, but Caleb and I couldn't bear to think of her leaving. Nevertheless, before long she moved out, leaving an even bigger void in our home.

You would think I would have been overwhelmed by a desperate need to be loved, but the truth was quite the opposite. I felt almost constantly as if I were immersed in love from people on each side of the veil. So many people were reaching out to us, sending us cards, offering us help, putting our name on the prayer rolls of temples all over the world and even on the prayer rolls of other religions! People were cheering, serving, and most of all, loving us. In many ways, I had never felt so loved in my life. What I needed so desperately at that time was to be able to love someone else. I almost felt that if I didn't find someone to share some of that overflowing love with soon, I was going to explode.

That's where things began to get complicated.

Without a doubt, I knew Caleb needed a mom. He needed someone who could give the kind of love and nurturing only a woman could give. But how could I ever dream of remarrying? I was sealed to Cheryl for time and all eternity, and my children needed to know I would never forget that. My marrying anyone else seemed to be out of the question for Clarissa. She seemed to think it would be disloyal or unfaithful, and she was always quick to remind me that I was *still married* and *always would be*. How could it *ever* be okay to give my heart to someone else? Trying to explain how it could be okay for me to open my heart and love another woman while still being in love with their mother seemed impossible. Honestly, it took a long time before the idea would even sit well in my own mind.

The thought of telling someone they were "the love of my life" or "my one true love" was overwhelming. I knew that if I couldn't say it sincerely, I should never say it at all. But that wouldn't be fair to my new wife—if, by some miracle, I could even *find* one. At the same time, if I *could* say it sincerely, I worried it would mean I was somehow unfaithful, which wouldn't be fair to my first wife. Meanwhile, the thought of being able to date any woman in the world was not exciting, like many men might think; it was *daunting*. After finding a needle in a haystack once, what were the odds of doing it again—especially when now you needed to use reading glasses to search for it? Besides, what kind of woman would want to compete with the memory of the one I was still so very much in love with?

That was my mindset as I tried to start over. I knew it was going to be hard. The truth is it was even harder than I thought. Finding a wife is a lot more complicated when you're forty-five years old and have kids!

Introducing yourself on campus to a girl in her early twenties is a great way to get a date if you're twenty-one and just off a mission. But doing it when you're forty-five doesn't stir the same feelings. It's more likely to make a girl want to call security!

So where is a middle-aged guy supposed to turn? Rarely would a woman my age attend a singles dance, so where did a guy find a wife when he's forty-something? I had spent half of my life with a woman who not only had true natural beauty but grace, charm, wit, substance, and testimony. I didn't want to get stuck with someone bitter, shallow, or incompatible.

I thought at first that it might be nice to find someone who had never been blessed with the opportunity of being married—some truly amazing person who, by some miracle, still happened to be out there just waiting for a kind, gentle, sincere man of steel and velvet to finally find her and sweep her off her feet. On the other hand, I worried about dating a person who had never been married. I couldn't help but wonder if maybe there was actually some good reason she was single. If there *wasn't*, I worried her circumstance might have made her bitter or caused her to hate men.

If a woman *had* been married, it was even *more* frightening. If she was divorced, I worried that it might be because she was ornery or hard to live with. But then, on the other hand, the divorce could have been her husband's fault because he had been unfaithful, abusive, or had left the Church. But then she might have huge psychological and emotional scars or serious trust issues.

If a woman was widowed, I was not only concerned about having to compete with a ghost, I also worried that she might be so absolutely wonderful that I'd fall desperately in love with her only to learn we could only be married "until death do us part."

To make matters worse, every woman out there had exactly the same kind of concerns about *me*.

Oh, how I missed the simple days!

In the end, it seemed the safest way to test the water would be through a dating website. I signed up for one specifically geared toward members of the Church. It felt a little odd trying to find someone to love in what basically amounted to an online mail-order catalog, but it did have certain advantages. From the pictures, I could see what each woman looked like before meeting her, so it was better than the blind dates my friends were always trying to set me up with. From their profiles, I could also learn all about them—their likes and dislikes, favorite foods and restaurants, music, hobbies, movies, sports, etc. The site also had a place for people to share information about how regularly they attended church, their calling, whether they held and used a current temple recommend, and so on.

Of course, I was always forced to assume the pictures on their profiles were *current* and that they were actually photographs of that woman. I met one woman who admitted she had used a picture that was taken eighteen years earlier and two others who were so self-conscious they tried using a picture of a sister and a friend! While some people tried to make themselves seem a little more interesting than they really were, if nothing else, at least I could tell whether they rooted for BYU or Utah. And as for their level of commitment to the gospel and their activity in church, my motto was always "trust but verify." I figured that if I ever got interested in anybody, it would be easy enough to call their bluff by going on a date to the temple.

I was selective about whom I contacted, and I went out very little but enough to help me realize that I really could learn to fall in love again. On the one hand, I realized I still needed time to heal, but at the same time, it became increasingly obvious that I would eventually have to "move on." For a quite a while, though, it seemed that all I was able to do was continue stumbling forward.

# 35
## A New Life

One day I was sitting at my computer looking through people's profiles when an amazing picture caught my attention. Caleb was sitting just a few feet away, composing a song on his synthesizer. I nudged him, pointed to the picture, and said, "Now *that's* the kind of woman I would like to marry!"

I had used those same exact words once before—when I first saw Cheryl. I was right both times.

Corrine Patricia Jensen turned out to be a treasure. She was everything I was looking for, although it took a while for me to realize it (and it took *her* even longer)! She was thirty-four years old, almost eleven years younger than me. While her age gave her a maturity and depth that many younger woman lacked, at the same time, her youth made her fun-loving and full of joy. She could play football with her boys in the cul-de-sac in the morning, go to the temple in the afternoon, and walk hand in hand with me on a stroll at sunset. We soon learned that we loved many of the same things, including—more than anything—our children and the gospel.

Corky, as I now call her, had been previously married for sixteen years and was the mother of four remarkable children. That might have scared a lot of men away, but for me it just made her all that much more attractive. My house had become too quiet, and I missed having a large family. The thought of marrying someone and having a full house right away sounded wonderful.

Corrine's divorce had been final for less than a week when I found her profile online. She had actually blocked everyone over forty. To this day, we don't how I was able to get through to her. Thankfully, I was.

Her oldest daughter's name was Rebecca. She usually went by "Becka," but sometimes her mom just called her "Boo." She was almost fifteen when Corky and I first started dating. She and her thirteen-year-old sister, Sarah, shared a room in their small three-bedroom bungalow in Saratoga Springs. Their two little brothers, Michael (ten) and Jonny (eight) shared the other children's room.

Divorce had been terribly hard for both her and the children. I could relate to what the kids were going through because I'd gone through a similar experience myself. One minute everything was fine; the next minute everything was over. One day you think you're part of a model family, sitting in church with your parents. The next day you're the product of a broken home, curled up in your closet screaming and crying.

The causes of the divorce were unknown to the children for the most part. Perhaps that was a blessing in many respects. But at the same time, it made the whole thing so unexpected and hard to understand.

Although she had been separated for nearly a year and a half, Corky had never dated or registered on any dating websites because she was still married. She was faithful, loyal, and true to the very last.

When she finally got word that her divorce was final, she immediately called her mother. Her mom and sister didn't even want her to get off the phone until they were sure they had talked her into at least "getting online and just looking." When she reluctantly agreed, they admitted they were already setting up a profile for her. She thought it was silly but consented, saying, "Okay, fine, but no picture. I'm waiting a year."

The Lord evidently had a different plan for her. She said that a few minutes later, she received a very strong prompting that told her, "Post a picture. You will not be any more ready in a year than you are now." She was surprised but—as she always does—followed the prompting. By the time she walked back to the phone and called her mother and sister to tell them it was all right to post a picture, they had already put it online. I am so very glad because the moment I saw it, I was hooked. Her warm, endearing smile made me feel like I had come home.

At first we were only sending messages to each other through e-mail and the dating website. Corky shared printed copies of some of those messages with her parents and others at a family reunion they had in Oregon, close to her brother's house. Spending much of their time at a remote lake, away from civilization, she was desperate to get online and see if I had written anything more. Her brother Kip made her a deal. She was absolutely terrified to ride a high zip line that ran over the water, but Kip promised he would give her a half hour of Internet access if she did. It took her thirty minutes to work up the courage, but she eventually braved the wild ride. She never looked down and has never looked back.

It was strange, but most of her brothers and sisters already knew a lot about me from the stories about the accident that had circulated on the news. They all got a big laugh out of the fact that I wrote such sappy, romantic letters to their sister, but at least they knew I was sincere.

The more we learned about each other, the more interested we became in growing our relationship. After writing for a while, we felt like we just had to meet. Late one Saturday evening, I drove across Utah Valley to meet Corky at her house. It was amazing how terrifying it was to anticipate getting together with her in person. I felt like I was in junior high again, wishing I could just have my best friend hand her a note that said, *Gary likes you. Do you like him back? Check yes or no.* But when we finally spoke face-to-face, it was amazingly comfortable. With her daughter Sarah as our chaperone, we went for a long walk and talked into the wee hours of the morning.

Soon after that, Caleb and I were invited over for dinner.

Now, in most of my profile pictures, I looked pretty much like I always had—clean shaven. But when Corky and I first met I was sporting a full beard. I had been acting in a movie for the Church as well as one of the Liken the Scriptures videos and was preparing to return to Hale Centre Theatre to play Bob Cratchit in *A Christmas Carol*. One of the first times I went to her house, I rang the doorbell, and her eight-year-old son, Jonny, opened it. When he saw me standing there, he thought I was a terrorist and wanted to slam the door and run into his room screaming. It was hilarious!

Caleb and I had dinner with Corrine and all of her children, and I began to learn what an enigma Corky was. In many things she demanded strict obedience, just as her mother and father had expected of her, but it wasn't uncommon to have wild water fights in her house, with glasses being dumped over people's heads, ice being put down Mom's back, and even the occasional threat of a garden hose if the kids ever got the upper hand. After dinner, I was eased into the tradition. What seemed to happen first was that everyone was required to help clean up. The discipline and work ethic of each of the young children was impressive. As soon as things were clean, though, a small water fight often seemed to break out. Sometimes it would turn into a hockey game, using brooms for sticks and the lid to the ranch dressing as a puck. It made scenes from movies like *Finding Neverland* and *Cheaper by the Dozen* seem pretty tame.

That seems like eons ago.

After months of dating, we were engaged on November 15, at my brother Dean's birthday. Not long after that, at Thanksgiving time, we went as a soon-to-be family to Disneyland. It was wonderful for all of us to be able to get to know each other and begin to bond. We had a fantastic time and made a lot of happy memories.

As we prepared for our wedding day, one of the first things we had to figure out was where we were going to live. Each of us was actually renting when we first met. We thought about buying the house that Corky lived in because it was just a few doors away from her sister Cheney. But as we thoughtfully considered it, we worried about it being too small. We were also concerned about how awkward it might be for Caleb and me to move in as "outsiders" to a ward and neighborhood where everyone else was already established. Our real hope was to find someplace that was new to all of us where we could all be on equal footing.

Since Caleb was homeschooled, his school would go with him wherever we went. That part was easy. In order to disrupt everyone else's life as little as possible, we wanted to keep Corky's four children in the same schools they were in. It was also important to keep them close to their cousins. In early December, we found a large house in Eagle Mountain that had never been lived in and decided to purchase it together. Corrine, Becka, Sarah, Michael, and Jonny moved in right away. Caleb and I looked forward to the day we could join them, when Corrine and I were finally married. We were anxious to become one big, happy family and start a new life.

# 36
## Very Happy Indeed

That same December, in 2007, the year after the accident, I returned to Hale Centre Theatre to reprise my role as Bob Cratchit in the twenty-fifth anniversary season of the play.

The audience of more than five hundred patrons was abuzz with eager anticipation as they settled noisily into their seats. Parents scrambled to gather children who had run out to the lobby for some last-minute treats. Senior patrons whose discipline and more settled lives allowed them to arrive early sat with warm smiles and calmly perused their playbills, learning what they could about each member of the cast. Couples, both young and old, having just come in from the frosty winter weather outside, snuggled together, enjoying each other's warmth and the charm of the theater's ambiance. On every side people chattered with excitement about presents they had just purchased, gift wrapping they had yet to do, and all of the sundry stresses and wonders the next day would hold. Newer patrons motioned around the theater in awe, pointing out piece after piece of the stunning scenery and props that had converted our theater-in-the-round into the streets of Victorian England. Bob Cratchit was getting ready to race in, late, to the office of Scrooge and Marley. I knew this, you see, because I was Bob Cratchit.

After my daughter Clarissa, my son Caleb, and I finished quietly warming up in the wings for the song in the opening scene, I tiptoed silently toward the stage. Parting the curtains of "vom 2"—one of the stage's three entrance corridors—just enough to make a hole the size of a quarter, I peeked out, making sure to remain unnoticed by the audience. Looking just beyond the stage, I scanned the crowd until I found my new soon-to-be family. There, a few rows from the top of the theater sat Corky, Becka, Sarah, Michael, and Jonny, eagerly waiting for the dimming of the lights that would signal the start of the play.

It always felt natural for me to play Bob Cratchit. Like the Cratchits, we were never rich, and at times, our feasts were very modest; but like the Cratchits, we were always grateful for whatever gifts the Lord provided. Our home was full of love, a place of warmth, joy, and peace. We ached and yearned, we read the scriptures together, we laughed, and we sang.

Each night as I performed the "happy Cratchit scene," I thanked my loving Father in Heaven for the sweet gifts of Christmas, the greatest of which was my family. When I performed the "sad Cratchit scene," I remembered all the blessed loved ones who had left this life and gone ahead. People often commented on how genuine my tears looked when, as meek and gentle Bob, I knelt before my child's grave. The previous year, those tears had flowed from dimming memories of five precious little ones I had buried, and they were dried by a loving wife who had endured those losses with me. Now, those old tears mingled with new ones that freely fell for those I had lost but a moment ago—Cheryl, Ian, and Julianna.

When life seemed hard and the tears just wouldn't seem to stop flowing, a wonderful new woman came into my life and assumed the role of Mrs. Cratchit. Once again a sweet and kind-hearted woman cheered and comforted me when she could and wept with me when she could not. And she was a good wife!

*Everybody knows that!*

Many kind people like Fred would enter our lives, filled with compassion and genuine goodness. Their Christlike love and countless acts of selfless service would bless our lives over and over. Opportunities of many kinds would come to each of us. Like Peter Cratchit, my child in the play, Clarissa would soon be "keeping company with someone and setting up for herself." Like Bob, I had always been so sure there was plenty of time to teach and prepare her, plenty of time before she was off to college or married. I had believed there was plenty of time to record music with Ian or play with Julianna or spend quiet moments of tenderness with Cheryl. But there was not.

Whenever I would pick up Tiny Tim's crutch and turn it sideways, it would remind me of a sword. Tears would immediately well up in my eyes as I remembered Ian lying in his casket. At times I would just stare at it and recall each of the poignant moments over the years that had caused me to plead in my heart, as Abraham once had, that a special child might be spared. And I'd relive the pain I felt each time there was no ram in the thicket for me and no angel came to stay my hand. Then, finally, I would kneel and surrender my heart to God and lay that crutch down as if it were on God's holy altar.

And I would remember what it felt like to lose our tiny twins. And Jordan. And Brianna. And Brayden. And Ian. And Julianna. And Cheryl. And I would look down into the tearing eyes of Caleb and Clarissa, who I *knew* were remembering them too. With their eyes they promised that they would not forget the ones who left us.

"Never, Father. Never."

Each night my heart, like Bob's, would swell with love and gratitude as I recognized all that I still had. And with a grateful heart, both on stage and off, I would wrap my arms around those two the Lord had left to comfort me. Knowing that they were still with me and they would never forget the many others who were not made me happy, very happy indeed!

# 37
## Joy in the Morning

Corinne and I were married on March 21, 2008. What a blessed day that was. The beautiful ceremony that sealed our love for time and all eternity was performed in the Mount Timpanogos Temple in American Fork, Utah.

Being blessed to marry Corky was a miracle! It was as if light poured into my dark and wounded soul, blessing me with a deeper understanding than I could have ever imagined of the words of the ancient prophet Alma, who testified of the great miracle the Savior had done in his life: "Yea, my soul was filled with joy as exceeding as was my pain."[92]

I thought back to the moment when I stood behind my totaled car. Everything seemed discouraging, overwhelming, and hopeless. Almost everything I treasured in this life had been taken from me. My wife was gone; my family was torn in half; my future looked bleak, sad, and lonely; my finances looked like they would be ruined; and I could not see a way out of the hole I was in. I never imagined that the Lord could help and heal me so completely and so quickly. He surely kept the promises He made and rewarded me manifold. The Lord has blessed me with an extraordinary life filled with treasured memories and an abundance of joy.

Without question, the happiest day of my life was the day I married Corky. The pain of my combined losses had carved out a huge hole in my heart. When Corky filled it, I came to know a whole new level of joy. In that magical moment, the Spirit bore witness to me of something I had known in my head but had never so poignantly felt in my heart: if I had never known that loss, I would have never known such gratitude. In an instant, love healed my heart.

On our wedding day, Corky was absolutely giddy. She was literally bouncing up and down as we sat on the couch listening to the sealer counsel with us before we knelt at the altar. It was wonderful to watch her parents as they watched her. It made them so happy to see *her* so very happy!

I marveled then and have understood even better since that on that day I didn't just marry an amazing woman; I married a whole amazing family. From the four wonderful children Corky brought to our family to Grandma and Grandpa Stannard, and from "Mom and Dad" to all of Corky's ten brothers and sisters with their families, the Lord has blessed me with a loving and righteous family that exceeded all my expectations and fondest dreams.

When Cheryl and I were married, only six people came to the wedding. My mother was the only family from either side that was able to be in the temple with us for our sealing. When Corky and I were married, the largest sealing room could barely contain everyone. And our family would keep growing.

Our wedding night was beautiful and sacred. We spent it at home, in our new house. Our wedding and reception had been beautiful. The gifts we received were wonderful. But for each of us, the most amazing gift was waking up in the arms of a loving spouse. We had each endured so much heartache, hardship, and loneliness. On so many nights, we had wet our pillows with our tears. This time our tears came in the morning, and they were tears of joy! It was wonderful to be reminded that trials don't last forever, but the blessings that come from them do. Psalms 30:5 says, "Weeping may endure for a night, but joy cometh in the morning."[93]

Of all the wonderful, boundless blessings the Lord sent to comfort me, restore my peace, and fill my heart with joy and gratitude, the greatest of them all was my wife. After enduring a long night of weeping, she was truly my joy in the morning.

# 38
## The End of Adversity

A LITTLE OVER A MONTH after Corky and I found our "happily ever after," Clarissa found love and healing as well. On April 23, 2008, she was sealed to Eric Brian Armstrong in the Salt Lake Temple.

Clarissa began a journey to try to become the kind of wonderful woman her mother was when she and Eric were blessed with two beautiful baby girls named Isabelle Julianna and London Athena. Caleb, meanwhile, had a new mom, who seemed to have been handpicked and tailor-made to help him become the very best he could be. He was also blessed to have a house full of brothers and sisters. Life was sweet again.

So did I live to finally see the end of adversity? Not hardly! In fact, we didn't have to wait long at all for trouble to track us down. It didn't even wait for a forwarding address; it found us on our honeymoon.

As soon as we had a date set for our wedding, I put a tremendous amount of effort into planning a perfect getaway for us. I booked a long cruise to the Western Caribbean—with stops in Cozumel, Mexico; Roatan, Honduras; Belize City, Belize; and more—followed by a week at the Epcot Center and the rest of Disney World. Corky seemed really excited, but she was probably a little worried given the horror stories she had heard about my first honeymoon.

Cheryl and I had also taken a cruise, but when the steward opened our cabin door, we stared in, bewildered. Instead of the two queen beds we were promised, the cabin had four *singles* (two upper and two lower) that were not even as wide as a pillow! We stood speechless, wondering how two people would ever fit on a bed that was too skinny for one, while the steward raved about the complimentary bottle of champagne on our nightstand. Before we even had time to ask if we could trade it in for a two-liter bottle of Sprite, we discovered that we had an even bigger problem. Our luggage was missing! We learned that it had only been checked to the Orlando airport and was stuck in an endless loop, going around a baggage carousel somewhere.

For the first couple of days, we tried as hard as we could to keep a low profile, but it was pretty difficult because I wasn't exactly sporting a typical cruise outfit. Had I been wearing shorts, sandals, and a flowered shirt, I might have remained pretty inconspicuous; unfortunately, I wasn't. Instead, I spent the first few days touring the beaches of the Bahamas in eighty-five degree weather, wearing a pair of jeans and a BYU football jersey. The first day people thought it was pretty cool. The second day they started looking at me like I was obsessed with football and never bathed. But by the third night, when I wore the same outfit to the *black-tie dinner* with the captain, they just thought I was stupid. Not even the fact that BYU had won the National Championship the year before did anything to add respectability to the outfit. I vowed I would never let anything like that happen again.

This time around I tried to be a little more prepared. When Corky and I packed for *our* honeymoon, we made sure to keep some extra clothes in our carry-ons. We arrived at the Salt Lake City airport early, but it was the day before Easter and the lines were so incredibly long that we ended up missing our first flight. But we still made it to Houston in plenty of time to catch the huge shuttle bus that would take us to the port in Galveston. Knowing we had all of our suitcases with us made the trip carefree and relaxing.

As the bus neared the port, a cruise representative stood to remind everyone to have their passports ready. I turned to Corky in a panic. I vividly remembered asking our travel agent if we would need passports. She told me, "No, you don't. The details of everything you need to bring will be in the cruise packet we send out to you." But the cruise packet didn't arrive until two days after we left.

I raised my hand and asked the lady on the bus if we had been misinformed. I was relieved when she answered, "No, no. That is technically correct."

I heaved a major sigh of relief, feeling like we had dodged a bullet. Had I seen the packet, I might not have been quite as shocked when she added, "All you need is a certified birth certificate."

As the bus pulled up to the dock, we pulled out our cell phones and started frantically dialing every friend and relative we could think of back home. All of our children and many of our brothers and sisters spent the next couple of hours rummaging through the filing cabinet and dresser drawers at the house Corky and I had purchased, while others went through the dozens of boxes that I had packed at my place in anticipation of Caleb and I moving in after the wedding. I told them exactly where I thought the document would be. It was the first place they looked, and in fact, I asked several people to check there again. Unfortunately, they never found it. It did eventually show up—six months later—in the very satchel beside my bed, where I had told everyone to look for it. It had been zipped up in a little secret compartment to keep it safe.

Anyway, back at the dock, we received word that someone had found Corky's birth certificate, and the authorities had accepted the faxed copy. Corrine was good to go! As we sat on our suitcases, waiting for a similar happy call about *my* documents, the ship's foghorn sounded the last call to board. I turned and looked at my new bride. The look on her face just broke my heart. Like a dolt, I tried to persuade her to go and enjoy the trip without me, but for some reason she seemed convinced that going on her honeymoon without her husband might somehow be less than completely satisfying. I was very grateful that she didn't leave on the cruise. Actually, at that particular moment, I was grateful she didn't leave, *period*.

We went outside and watched as the ship sailed away. While all of our shipmates were gleefully waving good-bye to the people on shore, we stood on the dock and waved to our shipmates. Admittedly, the "bon voyage" that we shouted to them was halfhearted. Personally, I was half hoping the ship would be boarded by pirates or sink so we could have some amazing story to tell our grandkids about how we had been spared just like the people who were fifteen minutes late to board the Titanic.

It was amazing for each of us to see how the other would respond to adversity. I suspect there are not many women who would have responded the way Corky did. She responded with love, kindness, understanding, and forgiveness—forgiveness that I felt I didn't deserve and could scarcely believe. After having a good laugh on the phone with her parents, we simply changed our plans. We spent the first few absolutely magical days of our honeymoon in Galveston, Texas, before going to Florida a week early. Our honeymoon turned out to be totally amazing! Most wonderful of all, we each got a glimpse of how the other would act if something major ever went wrong.

Not many months later, those skills would be put to the test in a much less humorous way. It was nearly impossible to believe, but somehow I found myself sitting outside the radiology lab of a hospital with my wife, while our daughter Rebecca was getting an MRI. I had spoken about similar experiences with Corrine many times, but never in a million years did either of us ever dream we would end up experiencing something like this together. After a half hour of waiting, the unimaginable happened; the radiologist came out and told us that Rebecca had a tumor in her abdomen the size of a softball. It was pretty ironic that it was Becka who ended up with a tumor. When she originally found out her mother was dating me, she insisted, "You can't marry *him*! Everyone in his family *dies*!"

Trying to comfort a wife who is suddenly confronted with the mortality of one of her children was an experience that seemed eerily familiar to me. This time though, the story had a happier ending. The tumor, which turned out to be benign, was completely removed. Becka healed quickly and went on to run cross country and track at Dixie State College, where she studied on scholarship.

From the very beginning, our marriage was one gigantic learning experience. Having four teenagers was hard enough by itself, but trying to raise them as part of a blended family was even more difficult.

We quickly learned that our parenting strategies were very different. Corrine was always thinking about the kind of person she wanted each child to become. She worked incredibly hard to build in her children exactness, strict obedience, a tireless work ethic, and the ability to do things for themselves. I was prone to take a softer approach and try to *love* the kids into submission. I didn't want to threaten them into helping Mom, for example; I wanted to teach them to truly love her enough and be selfless enough that they would *want* to serve her. If something needed to be done, I would often just start doing it, hoping my example of serving out of love would spread quickly. Occasionally I might have said something subtle like, "It looks like Mom could use some help in there!"

Caleb typically understood what I meant, but the others would just nod their heads and then go on doing what they were doing. They were accustomed to being given specific assignments and direct orders like, "Go help your mother with the dishes."

It was unnatural and felt mean to me to give mandates, but I soon learned that if I wasn't direct, the children would normally just ignore me.

From the day we first married, Corky and I have each been able to learn a great deal from the other. I started to see the benefits of doing things my wife's way, and she began to see some of the advantages of doing them mine. We've made tremendous progress. Now my kids respond well to her, not me, and her kids will listen to me but not her!

We found that certain of our children required a very specific kind of parenting, as did certain circumstances. Having a live-in example and mentor provided terrific on-the-job training and gave each of us access to a lot more parenting tools. I began to see that my way of doing things simply didn't work with the children my wife had brought into the family. Eventually I reluctantly admitted that some of my strategies didn't work on the ones *I* brought either. Learning from each other day by day, we have each tried to become a better parent.

Through every challenge, I've grown increasingly grateful for the person I married and the wonderful children we've been blessed with. They have made us proud in so many ways! All excellent students, four have already been offered college scholarships. Each of them has unique talents, like running, rock-climbing, drawing, writing music, singing, dancing, acting, playing football or baseball or basketball, wrestling, baking, sewing, peacekeeping, and negotiating, as well as humility, patience, innocence, obedience, faith, and courage. But more important than all of these things is the fact that they have brought us joy and honor by being examples of leadership and Christlike living. What they have *not* brought us is the end of adversity.

# 39
## Easier Doesn't Mean Better

As grateful as we were for the wonderful children we had each been blessed with, we very much wanted to have some together. We hoped it would unite us as a family. We didn't want to be an average blended family or even a *great* one; we didn't want to be a *blended* family at all. We just wanted to be a *family*. We didn't want "yours, mine, and ours"—just "ours."

We hoped for a honeymoon baby, but that wasn't to be. For the next couple of years, we continued to hope that a child was just around the corner. When that blessing didn't come, we each finally visited with doctors. Eventually we learned that Corky's progesterone was too low. Doctors put her on a medication called Chlomid, which the rest of us affectionately called "crazy medication." If I had to speculate on what was in Dr. Jekyll's transformation potion, my first guess would be Chlomid. We had been warned that one of its worst side effects was mood swings, but with Corky it sparked such fits of anger, rage, and hostility that no one could stand to be in the same room with her—not even me. Actually, I would highly recommend the drug . . . to someone who is looking for a 100 percent effective *birth control*! I personally believe that a naturally occurring strain of Chlomid is probably what causes some animals to *eat their young*!

Second, we realized that even if we *had* a child, there would be a twelve-year gap between that child and Jonny, our youngest. We decided to begin looking into adoption. Personally, my hope was that over time we would adopt a couple of younger children who could bridge the gap and provide continuity as we kept trying to have our own.

Around the same time, Corky read an article in the *Deseret News* about two Ukrainian orphan boys who had been part of a hosting program. An organization called "Save A Child" had been bringing over three to four dozen children a year to give them an American experience and to try to find families to adopt them. When she saw the article, she felt something special. She showed me the two-page story and we talked about it, but the whole idea had come about so suddenly that I was caught off guard. I couldn't imagine having children who didn't speak English. It was hard enough to deal with the ones we already had, who understood it perfectly.

For Corky, adoption was something very natural. She had been adopted herself. When she was nine, her birth father committed suicide. Her mother eventually married a wonderful man with two girls and a boy of his own, who loved and adopted Corrine and her six brothers and sisters. They were sealed in the temple a short time later.

To me, on the other hand, adoption was something very foreign. And *foreign* adoption was even more . . . well, *foreign*. I had nothing against foreigners; my own father came through Ellis Island. Ironically, he *did* have problems with foreigners. I used to laugh when he would rant about how immigrants were taking away American jobs. I occasionally had to remind him, "Umm, Dad, you *are* one of those immigrants!"

Like many people when they first consider adoption, I figured it would be a lot easier to adopt a newborn baby rather than an older child, and I wanted ours to be the first faces that baby ever saw. I imagined it was easier to raise them from infancy; I never wanted to hear one gripe, "I don't have to do what you say because you're not my 'real father.'" I thought it would be easier to adopt a child of the same race to avoid the stigma of having everyone know they were adopted. I assumed it would be easier to teach children who spoke the same language and easier to adopt only one rather than several. And I knew it would be easier to do a domestic adoption, since foreign ones cost nearly twenty times more.

I had so many concerns. I had no idea how badly children were treated in orphanages or what horrible things they might have been exposed to. I don't mean *little* things like scabies and lice, but *big* ones like reactive attachment disorder, post-traumatic stress syndrome, alcohol and drug addiction, pornography, promiscuity, and every conceivable form of horrific verbal, physical, and sexual abuse. Other alternatives just sounded a lot easier.

The moment I heard myself say the word *easier*, I realized I was being short-sighted and selfish. I learned long ago that wishing for what was easier was usually a mistake. Too many people use that word to justify or rationalize poor choices. How many times had someone asked me why I didn't choose something easier?

When I was trying to have children after losing several to cancer, people told me quitting would be much easier. When I fell in love with a woman with children, friends told me that marrying someone without them was easier. When I chose to forgive the drunk driver who killed my family, harboring bitterness and hatred was easier. Of course! It's also easier to lie, steal, drink, smoke, gamble, cheat, stay home from church, and not pay tithing. For that matter, why would anyone vote for the Lord's plan that required resisting temptations and enduring trials when Satan's plan of doing everything for us was so much easier? The answer to all of those questions is the same. *Easier doesn't mean better.*

Corky shrewdly left that adoption article sitting out in all sorts of conspicuous places. I don't know how many times I read it or stared at the picture of the two boys being held by the father of their host family. I saw that story in the bathroom, on the nightstand, tucked into the journal she wrote in every night, or marking a page in her scriptures. Little by little her cunning tactics worked, and my heart began to soften. After giving it a great deal of thought, we decided to participate in Save A Child's hosting program. Even then, the cost seemed so prohibitive that neither of us was convinced we would ever be able to actually adopt.

I remember visiting the home of Vern and Nanette Garrett, the couple who started the Save A Child foundation. The first time we met, Nan became a little emotional. There was a special connection between us. Like us, Nan had performed at Hale Theatre, as had several of her children. We learned that Nan's sister was Natalie Dowse, our neighbor in South Jordan and the mother of Ian's best friend, Ricky. What's more, our accident had happened just around the corner from the Garretts' house.

Nan told us all about their orphan hosting program and its origins. She shared the amazing stories about the wonderful Ukrainian children *they* had adopted, one of whom was serving a mission at that time. She even introduced us to two of them. It was amazing to hear their stories and see how well they were doing, how quickly they had picked up English, and what a beautiful and personable people the Ukrainians were. More intrigued than ever, we decided to look at the candidates to host.

Corrine had a strong impression we should host two boys and a girl, but she had never shared that with anyone. When Nan asked, Corky did tell her that we were "willing to consider a sibling set." Nan had already prayerfully picked children for us, hoping we might consider hosting them—two boys and a girl.

Older sibling groups like the one Nan was showing us were very hard for the orphanages to place. People rarely wanted older children at all, let alone more than one. As we looked at the pictures, there seemed to be pleading in their eyes. It felt like they needed us.

The girl, not quite twelve, had a typical Ukrainian beauty that was subtly masked by a facade of obligatory hardness that really seemed contrary to her sweet nature. In one picture, her arms were wrapped protectively around her two younger brothers, nine and seven. That picture gave the impression she had been forced to grow up too quickly. Nan read us a brief description written by the orphanage administrator about each child. She characterized them as obedient, helpful children who got along well with others. Nan said they were in good health, except that the youngest boy seemed to have a lazy eye.

"That's not a big deal!" I quipped. "We've got a few kids who are lazy from head to toe!"

As impressed as I was them, it was hard for me to think that someone else would be choosing children for us, even if they did it prayerfully, so I asked if there were other profiles we could look at. Nan was nice enough to allow us to peruse quite a number of them. The more we looked at, the more we felt drawn back to the three she had originally recommended. Each time we looked in their eyes, we seemed to fall more in love with them.

Nan told us that, because they were siblings, adopting all three of them would probably "only end up costing between forty-five and fifty thousand dollars," as opposed to the seventy-five thousand it would cost if they weren't. I looked at Corky. Only? With three children about to enter college and one about to leave on a mission, I couldn't imagine how we would ever be able to do it.

I turned to my wife and quietly whispered, "What's the point of hosting? We can't adopt them." What if we really liked them? What if they liked us? It would be cruel to get their hopes up if there was no way we could make them part of our family.

We told Nan that we loved the idea of adopting, we just didn't know how we could afford it. She flashed a knowing grin and said, "Boy, could I tell you stories!"

She had known a lot of people who felt the same way. Many of them ended up seeing major miracles that allowed them to actually adopt the children they had hosted. "If the Lord wants you to be together," she insisted, "things will work out—I promise you."

She left Corky and me alone for a while. After discussing it for some time, we chose to take a leap of faith, a giant step into the darkness. We decided to host them.

As we drove home, I wondered out loud, "What on earth did we just do?"

Corky tried to reassure me. "It's all right, honey. We're just *hosting* them."

We placed the pictures of the three children in the front of the large leather-bound copy of the Book of Mormon I used every morning to lead our family in scripture study. At times I would pull the picture out and look into the children's eyes. I felt like I had known them all my life.

We began to include them in our prayers. First, we prayed that we would be *able* to host them. We had to go through an extensive process. They scrutinized everything from my employment to the condition of our house, credit reports, taxes, background checks, details from our childhoods, letters from current and former friends and neighbors, recommendations and evaluations from family members, fingerprints, FBI and Interpol clearance documents, homeland security checks, you name it. After months of waiting and preparing, the day we were to meet the children finally arrived.

Dozens of nervous and excited families gathered at the airport for their first glimpse of the children who might very well end up changing their lives forever. The families were given colored balloons to differentiate the groups who were hosting children from each orphanage. The orphanages were designated by color because the names were too difficult to pronounce.

Some of the families there had hosted before, including quite a number who had already adopted. Some families were looking to adopt another child; others weren't hosting but had brought their child to help translate. Several media outlets also sent representatives to document what was happening.

After more than an hour of waiting, as the children and their adult chaperones made their way through customs, we caught our first glimpse of the children we would eventually know as Christina, Alex, and Jake.

Christina was a petite, poised, and caring girl with sparkling eyes. She was even cuter than we thought she would be, and I was surprised at how well dressed she was. She was very kind and nurturing to her brothers. In the orphanage they were inseparable. She always tried to keep them all together, and she worked hard to keep them safe.

Alex, her nine-year-old brother, seemed to be terrified at first. He walked timidly toward us, his hands in his coat pockets, his head bowed, and his face nearly hidden in the upturned collar of his coat. Corrine and I looked at each other, wondering if he had special needs. It turns out the only special needs Alex had were the same ones we all did—love, food, and a good night's sleep.

The littlest boy, Jake, seemed adorably vulnerable and very bashful, but before long the real Jake would emerge. He was a major goofball whose playful disregard for rules and others' personal space kept us perpetually exasperated and constantly laughing. To him every day was opposite day. We also learned he was a gifted pickpocket.

We couldn't even begin to imagine how intimidating it was for them to be in a country where they didn't speak the language. I remembered how hard it had been for me when I first arrived in Chile as a nineteen-year-old missionary, but these were children. As if all the different sights, sounds, customs, foods, and language weren't enough, they had to put up with being greeted at the beginning of what they were told was an "educational excursion" by a bunch of crazy couples who were acting like they already knew and loved them.

Most of the other families around us seemed to be in the same situation we were. They couldn't speak a word of Russian, and the children they were welcoming couldn't speak a lick of English. Even the simple chitchat like, "How was your flight?" typically used to end an awkward silence in such a situation became impossible. All we could do, for the most part, was stand around and stare at each other while we awkwardly waited for a translator.

The boys were tentative and scared half to death, but Christina helped them feel more comfortable. She seemed to have the confidence of a person who was well traveled. We learned later that for seven years, she had been going to southern Italy each Christmas and for four months every summer. She was only eleven but was fluent in Russian, Ukrainian, and Italian. I knew Spanish and some "Tarzan Turkish" (i.e. *me*, *food*) from living with my grandmother for six months before my mission, but neither of those languages seemed to be of much help.

The children couldn't speak our tongue and we couldn't speak theirs, but Corky was fluent in the one language that everyone understood—love. She smiled, gathered the three of them together, and wrapped them in her arms. They were actually here! After all those months of staring at their picture, they were here.

After about ten minutes—which felt like about ten months—we were finally introduced to Masha, a warm and bubbly translator who would be spending the first few days in our home.

What a blessing she was. We covered a few essentials, explaining who we were, introducing family members, telling them where the bathroom was, where our car was, and how long it would take to get home, then gathered our things and started to leave. While we waited outside the airport terminal for a shuttle to long-term parking, I tried my hand at another universal language—*play*. I picked up Alex and plopped him down in a wheelchair and promptly began racing him around, popping wheelies and making race car sounds as we weaved through all the others waiting for the bus to arrive. Next thing we knew everyone—American and Ukrainian—was smiling and laughing, and each of the children was begging for a turn. The time passed quickly, and the shuttle was there before we knew it to take us to our van.

For a guy who'd like to be driving a Mercedes McLaren, it was already hard enough to drive our Toyota Sienna, but for the three weeks we were hosting, we traded with our bishop. To have enough room for everyone, we were bebopping around Salt Lake in a twelve-passenger van. The whole way home, I kept pretending I was blowing the foghorn of an oil tanker. When we turned, I would wait until the front of the car was halfway down the road then ask if the back had turned yet.

Those three weeks were full of amazing, challenging, and hilarious experiences. For example, Ukrainians don't celebrate Halloween, and orphans don't typically get a lot of candy. On Christmas they get some chocolate, and that's usually it. The kids were incredulous when we first started explaining the holiday. It sounded amazing to them. In an attempt to teach them how trick-or-treating worked, Corky decided to play a little game with them the night before the actual holiday. She filled a large plastic bowl with candy then started going from room to room upstairs, pretending each one was her home. One by one, she had each child, dressed in all sorts of insane costumes, knock on a door or pretend to ring an imaginary doorbell, and she would give them candy. They picked up on the idea rather quickly and became instant fans.

We tried to teach them to say "trick or treat" and "thank you. Happy Halloween," but it was tough. The only words they knew when they came were *hi, thank you*, and the numbers from one to ten. Before long they were running around the house saying "tickle teeth," "chicka cheek," and "Hiehlo! Tenk yu. Heppy candy!"

I walked Christina over to my laptop, went into Google translator, and typed the English phrase "trick or treat" so she could understand what they were actually saying. She looked at the Ukrainian translation then stared up at me to see if I was joking. I couldn't understand why it would seem so strange to her. Out of curiosity, I copied the Ukrainian words and translated them back into English to make sure it had been translated correctly. When I saw what it actually said, I burst out laughing. According to the computer, "trick or treat" translated to "your wallet or your life."

I couldn't stop laughing for ten straight minutes! I ran upstairs to tell Corky and met her in the hall.

"Have you seen Jake?" she asked nervously.

"No. I thought he was with you."

With sudden fears of creating an international incident, we frantically searched for the seven-year-old. When we couldn't find him anywhere in the house, we decided to look outside, even though it was after eleven at night and freezing cold. We couldn't imagine why he would have ever gone out there. I went out the back door to see if he was on the trampoline. No luck. I walked back through the house to the front door. As I opened it, I heard Jake screaming over and over at the top of his lungs, "Chicka cheek! Chicka cheek!"

I looked toward the sound and, sure enough, found Jake, standing on the next-door neighbor's porch ringing the doorbell over and over again. Nobody answered. I was praying they were gone. I hastily herded him back inside, where Corky explained with words, charades, and ridiculously exaggerated hand gestures,

"Halloween tomorrow. No today. We go sleep—BIG sleep. Tomorrow we take shower, we eat, we do BIG work, then chicka cheek. You get BIG candy."

Don't ask me why she started talking like Tarzan; it just happened—and it didn't stop for a long time!

Somehow he understood at least part of what she was saying. After family prayer, which they couldn't understand, of course, everyone went to bed.

### He Can Heal

Early the next morning when I came down for family scripture study, the front door was wide open. Concerned, I rushed over and looked outside. I glanced over at the neighbor's porch, seriously hoping not see a diminutive little Ukrainian terror, but sure enough, there was Jake, ringing that same neighbor's doorbell again!

I ran to his side just as Ashley Romig came to the door. It was obvious he had gotten her out of bed. Too late to doorbell ditch her again, I stood beside Jake to explain.

"Ummm, hi, Ashley. I'm *so* sorry! He's really excited about trick or treating. Oh, and, ummm, by the way, that was him last night ringing your doorbell."

Surprisingly, she looked *relieved*. "Oh, thank heavens! My husband's out of town. When I heard the bell, I was sure it was the police coming to tell me he had been killed. I couldn't bear to answer it."

As the two of us were laughing, it occurred to me that Jake was no longer standing by my side. I looked over at our house to see if he was on his way inside. Instead, I caught a glimpse of him just as he came running from *another* neighbor's house carrying three bags of potato chips! If that wasn't enough, as soon as his brother and sister saw his stash, they insisted on going too. So before some people were even out of bed, Corky was taking them trick-or-treating through our kind but confused neighborhood.

For nearly three weeks, we had many similar moments of insanity as we hosted those three wonderful children. Those weeks were full of happy times. We all came to truly love them, and after a while they seemed to begin to trust and love us too. Of course, that was bittersweet, because we still never dreamed we would ever be able to adopt them.

The day before they left was Sunday. To try to make church more enjoyable for the children, we decided to attend a fast and testimony meeting in a Russian- and Ukrainian-speaking ward in Salt Lake City. The children were remarkably well behaved and surprisingly attentive as people stood and bore their testimonies. It seemed to help that most people were speaking in either Russian or Ukrainian. If ever someone stood and spoke in English, a kind, older Ukrainian woman would translate. As the meeting was about to end, Corky suddenly popped up and walked to the microphone.

Rarely have I heard such a powerful witness of the gospel of Jesus Christ. It was almost as if she was able to teach the entire message of the gospel in a few short minutes. Perhaps the most meaningful of all the powerful things she said were the words she ended with: "Mama loves you. I want each of you to know you are a child of God. And whether you decide to come and be part of our family or not, know that you have a Father in Heaven who loves you!"

What powerful words for an orphan to hear! The Spirit had obviously touched them. Their eyes were fixed on Corrine as she concluded her heartfelt testimony with simple eloquence. The Spirit in the room was magnificent. Many people were crying, and many, like me, were dumbfounded at the extraordinary thing they had just witnessed. I turned to Caleb and asked incredulously, "Did she just ask if they wanted to be *adopted*?"

Under the influence of the Holy Ghost, she *had*.

Every other member of the family felt they had already received their own personal answer about adopting, and we were all fasting that day for Corky to know if Christina, Alex, and Jake were meant to be part of our family. It seemed as if she had received her answer.

When the meeting concluded, several people came up to talk to Corky and comment on what an extraordinary spirit they had felt during her testimony. Many more came up to meet the children. The translator spent quite a bit of time having what seemed like a very serious conversation with the three of them. Since it was all in Russian, we had absolutely no idea what they were talking about.

When they were done, the translator turned to Corky and told her, "They said yes."

Corky looked at her, shocked, and asked, "And Christina . . . ?"

The translator smiled warmly, nodded in the affirmative, and answered, "Yes, Christina too."

We swept them up in our arms, and the rest of the family soon joined us in a huge group hug.

In an instant, our life was changed forever.

We spent some time at the Conference Center across the street and then toured Temple Square with a Russian-speaking sister missionary, who was also from Ukraine. We were pleasantly surprised and extremely impressed by how Christina could walk her younger brothers past murals from the Old Testament and the life of the Savior and explain every story to them. Alex seemed to know every story as well.

Finally, this good sister and her companion took us through a display that teaches that families are forever. It was so powerful for *all* of us. We were encouraged at how their eyes filled with light as they heard the good news of the gospel of Jesus Christ.

The next morning it was time for them to return to Ukraine. It was an incredibly emotional experience. After family prayer, Jake got up and ran back up to his bedroom. He grabbed the panda bear Caleb had given him, curled up on his bed, and started sobbing. Our hearts just broke as we saw how he suffered. He had never known what a family was. He was only one year old when he was sent to the orphanage. That was all he ever knew. Now, after finally getting a taste of what it meant to have a family, it was being ripped away from him, and his little heart was breaking.

When we finally arrived at the airport, most of the orphan children were happy and excited to see their friends and anxious to share stories about all their adventures. I'm sure many of them were also eager to return home to the food and customs that were familiar to them. Some of the families were probably eager to go back to communicating without charades too.

We just held our children and cried. Through his sobs, poor little Jake just kept repeating, "No Ukraine. Yes Mama. Yes America. No Ukraine."

We didn't want them to go, but we had no choice. It was mandated in the hosting agreement that all the children had to go back, even if the hosting family wanted to adopt them. All our hearts were breaking. We knew it would cost a small fortune to get them back and it would probably take six months to a year to do it, if we even could, but in our hearts we felt like they were already part of our family. It felt like we were sending our children to complete strangers to live in who-knew-what-kind of environment. We had to find a way to bring them home.

This was exactly what we had feared, yet somehow we were no longer afraid of it; we were driven. We *loved* them. If that wasn't amazing enough, they loved us too!

It was torturous to watch them leave. Just when all of us finally seemed to be on the same page and we were all beginning to get our hopes up, we had to let them go. Saying good-bye was very hard because we knew it would take a miracle for us to ever see them again.

It would have been so much *easier* if we had just chosen not to host them. But once again we could see that easier doesn't mean better.

# 40
## More Than the Beginning

The next few months were filled with miracles. People in our ward and neighborhood rallied around us. One dear friend, Amy Kawa, spearheaded the largest yard sale we had ever seen. Mandy Bradshaw organized a giant bake sale. Two of our daughters, Sarah and Becka, sponsored a 5K race and fun run. They had to handle city permissions, road signs, mile markers, timers, awards, race T-shirts, and securing sponsors, but they did it all masterfully and with joy. Friends like Peter Breinholt, Cheri Call, Joe Paur, Aaron Edson, the Garretts, and Jennie Bezzant (Mrs. Utah) put on a benefit concert. The whole family went door-to-door, first peddling Papa Murphy's pizza cards and Smoothie King cards, then later selling printed copies of a drawing Caleb had done of President Monson.

Our son Michael had a special experience selling those pictures. Our whole family went to watch Becka and Sarah run in a track meet in Kearns. While we were waiting for their events, Michael decided to try to sell a few of the portraits. With a goal in mind of selling five, he walked around the stands offering them to people. Michael not only met his goal but came back with $125. One of the men who bought one of the drawings had tracked him down a little while later and handed him a hundred dollar bill.

"This is for the adoption," he said.

Before Michael could even thank him, the man hurried off. Excitedly, Michael ran to tell Corky what had happened. She asked him to point the man out so she could thank him. When he saw her coming, he tried to turn away, but she was eventually able to thank him. She asked, "Why would you do that? You don't even know us."

The man pointed to heaven and replied, "No, but *somebody* does. And when He speaks, I listen."

Lightstone Studios, who had helped us so much after the accident, wanted to help with the adoption too and donated boxes of "CeranAid" CDs for us to sell. Many others helped as well. Children from the neighborhood made and sold jewelry. Corky's brother Todd set up a website called "UkrainianMiracle.com." Her brother Kip and his family took on a massive family fund-raising project they called "Cousins for Christmas." Among other things, they sold soldering irons on eBay and even donated a portion of their tax return. Little Lindsay Snider, the six-year-old daughter of a former counselor in our bishopric, decided to put together a bake sale in the garage of their home in Pleasant Grove. Here is a portion of what her parents wrote on their family website, Sniderfamily.com, about the shocking contribution their young daughter made.

> The total amount Lindsay gave the Cerans was an astonishing $3,855.70! When we delivered the money to the Cerans, Corrine told me that while the total amount they needed was around $50,000, a lot of that was administrative fees and fees to different agencies and people. The official adoption fees totaled $16,000—$8,000 for the first child and $4,000 each for the other two. So I was able to explain to Lindsay that her efforts essentially paid the adoption fees for one of the children.

After Corky and I had been in Ukraine for more than a month, we had our official court date on April 6. We were well prepared for the hearing, yet we were still terrified. The judge was a stern and serious man, and he remained that way throughout most of the proceeding. After grilling me first, then my wife, he decided to interview each of the children. One wrong answer from any of us could cause him to decide against us, and if he did, that was that; his decision was final, and there could be no appeal. I was especially worried when he got to Jake. Let's just say our little "Jakester" can be quite the jokester, and sometimes he can be a little bit of a loose cannon.

Judge Shevchenko looked sternly into Jake's face and asked him in Ukrainian, "Do you know why you're here?"

I prayed like mad he would not say something rude.

Jake just stared at him, seeming totally intimidated, and shook his head side to side. We looked at each other and then at Yana, our facilitator, in horror. We had gone over all this. He knew why we were there. We were trying to get the judge's permission to make the three children part of our family. Just as we were getting really worried, Jake smiled as only he can, stood up tall and proud, and shouted, "We're being adopted!"

The judge grinned for the first time in the proceeding. He quickly caught himself, put his grumpy face back on, and asked in a serious and self-important way, "Do you realize who I am?"

Jake seemed frightened by his tone of voice and his serious demeanor. He looked at this man, all dressed in a suit, surrounded by Ukrainian flags, then gulped and said, "Yes, you're the president."

The judge—and everyone else in the courtroom—burst out laughing and couldn't stop for several minutes. When he finally managed to control himself again, he wiped away the tears he had rolling down his cheeks from laughing so hard and pointed to the court reporter, the representative of the Division of Child Services, and the representative of the orphanage. "That's right, young man. And this is my cabinet." Then he laughed for another few minutes. Jake had won the judge's heart.

When he was done, Corrine and I each stood to make our final petition, which basically said, "Your Honor, we respectfully ask you to approve our petition to adopt, to authorize the Russian Federation to issue new birth certificates, listing myself, Gary John Ceran, and my wife, Corrine Patricia Jensen Ceran, as the children's parents, and to order that the children's names be changed to Christina Marie Ceran, Alexander Jensen Ceran, and Jacob Gary Ceran."

After adjourning for a twenty-minute recess that would have seemed like an eternity had it not been for Jake, the judge returned and issued his ruling. The children were officially ours!

After four long but wonderful weeks in Ukraine, we returned home with some amazing memories and an approved adoption—but without the children. More steps were required to get their Ukrainian adoption recognized by the government in Russia, where they were born. They had to have new Russian birth certificates issued with their adopted names in order to get new Ukrainian passports so they could travel to America. Our facilitator's son, who was enlisted to go to Russia to help, said he had only faced situations like this twice before. Once, it took two months to resolve; the other time it took almost a year! Thankfully, ours took only a few weeks. Within a month we were back in Ukraine ready to take them home.

Looking back, it's hard to believe all that's happened. By the time I was forty-five, the Lord had taken seven of my nine children and my wife. Who would have ever dreamed that He, in His infinite mercy and loving kindness, would heal my heart, send me a wonderful new wife, and bless me with seven more children? He gave me love and hope, and He filled my heart and home with love.

On November 4, 2011, we were blessed to go to the Salt Lake Temple so that Christina, Alex, and Jake could be sealed to our family for time and all eternity.

I think back to the accident. As I stood behind my car, I felt like the Israelites at the Red Sea, staring at what seemed to be an insurmountable obstacle; like the disciples who were afraid they would perish on a stormy sea, I saw no escape; and like Joseph Smith in the Sacred Grove, I was "ready to sink into despair and abandon myself to destruction"[94] because I was overcome with feelings of helplessness and hopelessness. Only then, when I was finally willing to admit to God that I couldn't make it without Him, was He able to begin to show His power. In my most desperate moment, I could not have begun to imagine the miracles He had in store to bless me!

I marvel at the wondrous things the Lord has done in my life. I am grateful for all the marvelous truths the Lord has taught me through my trials. I thank Him for the love in which He has engulfed me, and I pray that I will have the strength to become the man those trials were intended to help me to become.

I remember a moment in the hospital hallway, after the accident, when my brother put his arm around me and said, "Gar, I used to think you were a lot like Job. The only difference was that Job's story had a *happy* ending. You know, Gar, this time I think it's going to be different!"

And it certainly has been. The Lord has given me everything I lost and more. He has answered each moment of sorrow with joy, a hundred fold, and has allowed my life to have a storybook ending: "And he lived happily ever after . . ."

As I look back with hindsight's clear vision and see the mercy and loving kindness that are now so evident in the plan Heavenly Father had for me, I marvel at how good He has been! Through painful losses and a merciful and miraculous restoration, He has helped me to become truly grateful for every blessing. He has filled my life with purpose, my quiver with children, my heart with joy, and all my days with the love of a beautiful, growing family.

Their warmth has comforted me, their smiles have cheered me, and their zany antics have kept me constantly laughing. But above all this, their *love has healed my heart.*

From time to time, I have sat and reflected on the extraordinary experiences the Lord has used to shape my life. When I think of my own trials and those of so many around me, it amazes me how the gospel of Jesus Christ allows each one of us to endure so many heart-wrenching trials and still *smile!* It is one of life's great wonders.

At times, we all, as people of faith, are driven to our knees to plead for one we love to be healed. Sometimes they are, and *that* is a great wonder. Other times we pour out our hearts to God only to watch in agony as those we love falter and die. When such a loss makes one's spirit and one's sorrow sweeter—not more bitter—and when their faith not only stays strong but actually *grows* in such a tragic circumstance, it is another of life's great wonders!

The Lord has blessed me with experience, knowledge, and joy beyond anything I had ever known. My Father in Heaven has favored me with more than I ever had before. Truly He did for me the same wonderful thing He had done so many years before for His faithful servant Job; He blessed the latter end of my life with even "more than the beginning."[95]

# He Can Heal
## by Gary J. Ceran

Of all the wonders in this world
The greatest of all I knew sought I
For in my arms my boy, my girl,
And sweet wife were about to die.

In stunning stillness, steeped in death—
My spirit troubled and confused—
I prayed for strength and living breath,
*For them . . . and* us; *these words I used:*

Upon my knees, yea face to dust
I seek Thy comfort, found above,
And plead for peace—Oh, Lord, I must
Be strengthened by Thy boundless love!

Thou knowest how my soul is aching;
*Who more than* Thee *this pain could know?*
Dear God, my quivering heart is breaking
Please *bless me this one thing to know:*

Thou sayest that through administrations
We may draw on Thy great powers
If death be not one's ordination
And if sufficient faith is ours

Oh, is my faith sufficient, Lord
That these deep yearnings of my soul
Can bring Thy finger or Thy Word
To bless and heal and make us whole?

*Yea* us, *for are we not* all *ailing*—
Fleeing death, yet ever near it?
Every *life is frail and failing* . . .
Some in body, some in spirit.

While some seek health, some make confession,
But all *petition greater strength,*
For we all require Thy intercession,
If we're to be made whole at length.

Oh, Lord, who made both Earth and skies,
Thou, God, Omnipotent, Omniscient,
My King, Most Merciful and Wise,
I beg Thee, make my faith sufficient!

*I BELIEVE!* . . . *But help Thou mine unbelief*
And I shall walk upon the water!
But if, as Peter, I seek relief,
Lord, save my wife and son and daughter!

Behold their lives, lain on the altar . . .
*As Isaac's life, Lord,* theirs *we give;*
We offer all, though our hearts falter,
Pleading "Stay thy hand and let them live!"

Oh, must we drink this bitter cup
That we might comprehend thy Son?
If so, behold, we drink it up;
Thy will, O Lord, not ours be done!

Then came His voice—I still can hear it—
Making known His mind, His will,
His love, His peace . . . His very Spirit!
Yea, I knew God as I was still.

N' there, on my knees, I felt His power
*And oh, what* wondrous *things I learned!*
For He was with me that very hour,
And upon my heart, these words He burned:

Though lame should walk, or blind should see
*Or* dead *men* rise and be made whole,
*The* greatest wonder of all, *said He*
Is the salvation of the human soul!

Though all God's wonders doth astound me
The greatest yet I scarce could tell
Though miracles were all around me,
He'd wrought one in my soul as well!

My loved ones died but live once more,
For Christ hath saved us from the Fall!
And we've the peace we pleaded for;
For our Savior's love engulfs us all!

And now I see in this refining moment
His purpose, yea, the reason why . . .
And I know, through His divine Atonement
*They all* were *saved . . . and so was I!*

With all my heart I humbly share
A testimony sure and true
He knows your pain; He hears your prayer
And someday He will rescue you.

The greatest joy you'll ever know
And the sweetest peace you'll ever feel
Will come once trials have helped you grow
And proved to you that He Can Heal!

I prayed for healing that Christmas, and in ways I never expected, my family and I were healed. I prayed for salvation that Christmas, and in different ways all six members of my family were saved. I prayed for a Christmas miracle only to realize it had already come: "For God so loved the world that he gave his only begotten Son, that whosoever believeth in him should not perish, but have everlasting life."[96]

May the hope that comes from the life and sacrifice of our Savior, Jesus Christ, calm your fears and comfort you in your time of need. May you discover the peace that comes from understanding and allow your life to be *blessed* by adversity.

It is said that "life is like a grindstone, and whether it grinds a man down or polishes him up depends on the stuff he's made of."[97] Adversity is the seedbed of true testimony and the proving ground on which the Lord reveals us to ourselves. Through trials He helps us to discover who we really are, what we really know, and who we truly love. Then, through His Atonement, He helps us to be much more, know much more, and love much more than we ever thought was possible.

So when you feel your life is tormented by troubles or plagued with pain, when you are afflicted by the anguish of adversity or you are longing for a lasting love, when you are left lamenting the loss of a loved one or are struggling to survive the sorrow of sin, when *whatever* load you carry seems too great to bear—cast your burdens on the Lord. He is aware of your trials and your limitations; He knows your pain and how much you can bear. He hears your prayers, but he also knows your thoughts and desires and needs. The Lord offered His peace to the suffering, saying:

> Lift up your heads and be of good comfort . . . I will ease the burdens which are put upon your shoulders, that even you cannot feel them upon your backs . . . ; and this will I do that ye may stand as witnesses for me hereafter, and that ye may know of a surety that I, the Lord God, do visit my people in their afflictions.
>
> And now it came to pass that the burdens which were laid upon [them] were made light; yea, the Lord did strengthen them that they could bear up their burdens with ease, and they did submit cheerfully and with patience to all the will of the Lord.[98]

He makes and keeps that same promise to us today.

If you ever feel your prayers are falling on deaf ears or, like Lazarus's sister, you cannot understand why He is slow to answer you or seemingly does not come in time, do not doubt. If the Lord ever denies a blessing to one who pleads in righteousness and faith, it is so He can provide an even greater blessing later. If your miracle has not yet come, trust Him and become "as a child, submissive, meek, humble, patient, full of love, willing to submit to all things which the Lord seeth fit to inflict upon him, even as a child doth submit to his father."[99] If you do, you will be blessed to see even greater miracles than the ones you sought.

Even in my hardest trials and darkest times, the Lord has never forgotten me. He will never forget *any* of us. He said, "Can a woman forget her sucking child, that she should not have compassion on the son of her womb? Yea, they may forget, yet will I not forget thee. Behold, I have graven thee upon the palms of my hands."[100]

Elder David A. Bednar, a special witness of the Lord, Jesus Christ, taught of the scope and power of the Lord's sacrifice in a powerful recent conference talk entitled "The Atonement and the Journey of Mortality."

The scope and magnitude of the Savior's suffering in Gethsemane and on Calvary is unfathomable. Jesus not only suffered for our sins but for our sorrows. To descend below all things, He had to bear the burden of every physical and emotional weakness or pain that any us would ever experience. He took upon himself the anguish of every sinner—not only the harrowing remorse of the penitent, but the torturous guilt of those who don't repent. Christ felt the pains of all the brokenhearted. He endured the turmoil of the vile abuser and the heartache of the innocent abused. He felt the pangs of a poor man's hunger and the emptiness of the selfish rich. In fine, He took upon Himself all of our stresses, fears, and illnesses, our disabilities, failures, and physical suffering, and the burden of every inequality, injustice, and persecution that any one of us would ever suffer. Because he bore that incomprehensible weight, the Savior knows perfectly and understands exactly what we feel, when no one else can. With perfect empathy, He provides perfect relief. His power to heal us has only one limit—our willingness to accept the gift that He freely offers us. Alone, there are burdens we could never bear, suffering we could not endure, and sorrow from which we could not heal, but with God nothing is impossible.[101]

I testify that if you ask the Lord in faith to apply the Atonement in your life, your suffering will be swallowed up in His. He will help and heal you. Either He will carry you through your trials or He will bless you with the strength to carry yourself through them.

I not only believe in miracles, I depend upon them. I have been blessed to experience so very many. Whenever I have reached the limits of my endurance, in those desperately overwhelming moments when I felt like I simply could not go on, the Lord has always come to rescue me and has provided the blessed relief I so desperately longed for. I testify that the Lord will always be there for you. When it seems like all is lost and life is hopeless, take courage, stand firm, and trust in the Lord's love and mercy. There is always hope in Him! You will be happy again.

May my experience be a comfort and a witness to you in the darkest hour of your personal affliction that those miracles, that hope, and those happier days will surely come. And may the merciful, miraculous way in which our loving Savior rescues each one of us not only *from* our trials but also *through* them bear a solemn testimony, to which I add my own, that *He can heal.*

# Endnotes

1. In Neal A. Maxwell, *We Will Prove Them Herewith*, (1982) quoting Annie Swetchine, 123.
2. Emily Dickinson, *The Complete Poems of Emily Dickinson* (Boston: Little, Brown, and Company, 1924).
3. Isaiah 53:3.
4. Richard Wilkins and Barlow Bradford, Hale Centre Theatre Script for *A Christmas Carol* (Adaptation created in 1982), 40.
5. Charles Dickens, *A Christmas Carol*, Cleartype Edition (New York, Boston: Books Inc., late 1800s), 71.
6. Wilkins, Bradford, 40.
7. Ibid.
8. Ibid.
9. Ibid.
10. Dickens, 71.
11. Ibid., 72.
12. Ibid., 72.
13. Ibid., 71.
14. Wilkins, Bradford.
15. Ibid., 41.
16. Dickens, 72.
17. Ibid.
18. Ibid.
19. Ibid.
20. Ibid.
21. Wilkins, Bradford, 41.
22. Dickens, 72.
23. Ibid., 73.
24. Ibid.
25. Ibid.
26. Ibid.

27. Ibid.
28. Wilkins, Bradford, 41.
29. Ibid.
30. Ibid.
31. William C. Dix, 1837–1898, "What Child Is This?"
32. Dickens, 82.
33. Clement Clarke Moore, *The Night before Christmas* (Houghton Mifflin Harcourt, 2005).
34. Doctrine and Covenants 121:7.
35. Alma 48:17.
36. Dunn and Eyre (quoting Edwin Markham), 41.
37. Greg Kofford, address given at the funeral of Cheryl Lynne Ceran, Ian James Ceran, and Julianna Janae Ceran, December 30, 2006.
38. John Taylor, *Journal of Discourses*, 24:197.
39. http://thinkexist.com/quotation/talents_are_best_nurtured_in_solitude-but/197570.html.
40. Author unknown, English traditional Christmas carol published by William B. Sandys in 1833.
41. http://www.imdb.com/title/tt0309912/quotes.
42. Chris Frazier, "EMT of the Year Recalls Tragedy of Christmas '06," *Salt Lake Tribune*, June 21, 2007.
43. EMS Tribute—Joseph Treadwell Delivers His Utah EMT of the Year Award Acceptance Speech, http://www.oberlin.edu/faculty/svolk/citation.htm. May 21, 2007.
44. Proverbs 17:17.
45. Zack Van Eyck, "Crash Claims Mom, 2 Children," *Deseret Morning News*, December 25, 2006.
46. Mosiah 18:9.
47. Chris Williams, letter to author, May 25, 2007.
48. Chris Williams, *Let It Go* (Salt Lake City: Shadow Mountain, 2012), front inside dust cover.
49. Ben Winslow, Pat Reavy, and Wendy Leonard, "Mall Massacre—Gunman Kills 5, Wounds Others before He's Slain," *Deseret Morning News*, February 13, 2007, 1.
50. Pat Reavy, "Crash Victim Issues a Call for Forgiveness" *Deseret Morning News*, February 13, 2007, 1.
51. Elaine Jarvik, "A Year of Forgiveness," *Deseret Morning News*, December 28, 2007.
52. See James E. Faust, "The Healing Power of Forgiveness," *Ensign*, April 2007.
53. Dr. Seuss, *How the Grinch Stole Christmas* (New York: Random House, 1957).
54. Dr. Seuss, 165.
55. Doctrine and Covenants 137:10.
56. http://www.elvish.org/gwaith/movie_inscriptions.htm#anduril.

57. Mark 4:39.
58. See Moisés Nefi Morales Gonzáles, "I Know Families Can Be Forever," *Ensign*, January 2007.
59. See Spencer W. Kimball, *The Teachings of Spencer W. Kimball* (Salt Lake City: Bookcraft, 1982), 38–39.
60. Hebrews 12:6, emphasis added.
61. Dunn and Eyre (quoting Elder Orson F. Whitney), 40.
62. Ibid. (quoting Wilford Woodruff), 42.
63. The Westminster Collection of Christian Quotations, Google Books, http://enq.translatum.gr/wiki/Charles_Spurgeon.
64. Dunn and Eyre, 15.
65. Doctrine and Covenants 122:5–8.
66. 1 Peter 2:20.
67. Dunn and Eyre (quoting Rossiter W. Raymond), 16.
68. Ibid. (quoting an unknown author), 16.
69. Ibid. (quoting John Taylor), 16.
70. Doctrine and Covenants 121:7–8.
71. Dunn and Eyre (quoting Rabindranath Tagore), 12.
72. Ibid. (quoting unknown author), 14.
73. Ibid., 33–34.
74. Ibid., 33.
75. Revelation 3:20.
76. Minnie Haskins, "The Gate of the Year," in *The Desert*, 1908.
77. Proverbs 3:5–6.
78. John 14:27.
79. Doctrine and Covenants 84:88.
80. Dunn and Eyre (quoting J. R. Miller), 18–19.
81. Alma 26:11–12.
82. Doctrine and Covenants 64:9–10.
83. Alma 44:6.
84. Chris Williams, *Let It Go* (Salt Lake City: Shadow Mountain, 2012), 97.
85. Ibid., front inside dust cover.
86. Matthew 7:2.
87. See Richard G. Scott, "Healing the Tragic Scars of Abuse," *Ensign*, May 1992, 33.
88. Matthew 5:38–39, 42–48.
89. Alma 40:11–12.
90. 3 Nephi 17:17.
91. See Meredith Wilson, "May the Good Lord Bless and Keep You," (1950).
92. Alma 36:20.
93. Psalms 30:5.
94. Joseph Smith—History 1:16.
95. Job 42:12.

96. John 3:16.
97. http://thinkexist.com/quotes/josh_billings/2.html.
98. Mosiah 24:12–15.
99. Mosiah 3:19.
100. Isaiah 49:15–16.
101. See David A. Bednar, "The Atonement and the Journey of Mortality," *Ensign*, April 2012.

## About the Author

GARY J. CERAN WAS BORN in New York and raised in New Jersey. He served in the Chile Concepción Mission and later married Cheryl Lynne Smith. The two were blessed with nine wonderful children. This book describes just a few of the trials and traumatic events that ultimately led to Gary's burying seven of those nine children and his wife.

Brother Ceran graduated from Brigham Young University with a degree in finance. He worked for seventeen years as an accountant and senior financial analyst in the Finance and Physical Facilities Departments of the Church, most recently with responsibility over its headquarter facilities and historic sites. He left Church employment in 2004 to serve as president and CEO of New Legacy Capital Ventures Inc. He subsequently served in other executive positions and in consulting and sales. He is currently employed as a director with Unicity International.

In 2008 Gary was blessed to begin a new chapter of life with his beloved wife, the former Corrine Patricia Jensen. Corrine added four children to his remaining two. In 2011 the couple adopted three children from Ukraine. He once again has a beautiful wife and nine children.

His firesides and motivational speeches have touched many lives. It is his hope and prayer that this book will do the same and bring perspective, peace, and comfort to all those who are suffering.